BUSES

YEARBOOK 2022

Edited by ALAN MILLAR

BUSES
YEARBOOK 2022

FRONT COVER: *The first three-axle double-decker to operate on a London bus route since 1962 is Go-Ahead London TA1, a hybrid BCI built in China.* MARK LYONS

PREVIOUS PAGE: *The last double-deckers acquired by Whippet were 17 Volvo B7TLs with Wright Eclipse Gemini bodywork new to First London and transferred from then parent company Tower Transit in 2015. Their departure in 2020 made Whippet all single-deck for the first time since 1955 (see p52).* JOHN ROBINSON

BACK COVER (UPPER): *March 2002 and Yorkshire Terrier 1738 (POG 586Y), an MCW Metrobus MK2 new to West Midlands PTE, leaves the Meadowhall Interchange on the northern outskirts of Sheffield. The enclosed footbridge above linked bus and coach routes, along with the Stagecoach Supertram and two individual sets of railway platforms (see p98).* TONY WILSON

BACK COVER (LOWER): *The sole Optare Excel operated from new as a route bus in Malta was converted from automatic to manual transmission (see p90).* JOHN YOUNG

Published by Key Books
An imprint of Key Publishing Ltd
PO Box 100
Stamford
Lincs PE9 1XQ

www.keypublishing.com

ISBN: 978 1 80282 032 4

Printed in Malta by **Melita Press**
Paola. Pla 3000
Malta. Europe

www.keybuses.com

Fleetline heaven. In the mid 1980s, parts of the West Midlands were awash with the type, as here at the bus station in Dudley, in the shadow of the Norman castle (see p74). LAURENCE KNIGHT

Fifty years on

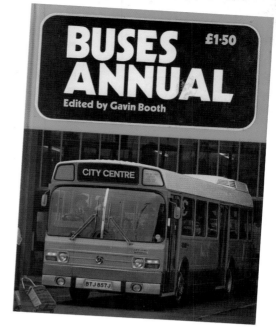

Welcome to this latest *Buses Yearbook* and if, as legend has it, this is an eagerly requested gift you are reading for the first time on Christmas morning, then let me wish you the compliments of the season.

The *Yearbook* first appeared in 1963 as *Buses Annual 1964*, dropped the *Annual* name from the editions dated for 1968 to 1971, and has been *Buses Yearbook* since the 1989 edition. This is the 50th anniversary not only of it returning as *Buses Annual* but also of its transformation by a dynamic young editor.

A then 28-year-old Gavin Booth, whose anthology of stories titled *Bus Stop* had set a new standard of what a government minister described recently as "bus literature", made the *Annual* bigger and brighter, packed with articles and photo features on topics ranging from the latest developments back to prewar days.

Gavin steered the *Annual* through a total of 15 editions before handing over to our mutual friend Stewart J. Brown who has now decided after an admirable stint of 35 years that he also wants to spend more time doing different things. By agreeing to edit this edition after stepping down from over 21 years as editor of *Buses*, I may have reinforced the conviction of a commissioning editor at our previous publisher that the three of us were what he called a "Scottish Bus Mafia", but trust that the variety of content this year shows that our interest in bus activities takes in a great many places beyond our doorsteps and birthplaces.

I'm delighted that, along with contributors *Buses Yearbook* has picked up in the intervening years and some newcomers, two of the authors of articles in the 1972 edition have willingly written for this one.

Gavin is one of them. Fifty years ago, he described the razzmatazz of buses and coaches at motor shows and illustrated the book's cover with a prototype Leyland National posed in the new Preston bus station. It's fitting that this time he has dipped into his large collection of manufacturers' publicity photographs, some collected at shows, and that the subject of one of them also was posed in that bus station, pretending to be somewhere else.

The other is the incomparable Robert Jowitt, who first appeared in print in the 1972 *Annual* and has been in many editions since. He returns this year with his unique writing style and creative photography, which has surely inspired others to compose pictures showing more of the environment in which vehicles are working.

Just as 50 years ago, we look forward as well as back in this edition. The Leyland National has gone from being a bus of the future to a significant piece of bus heritage. The future today looks electric and is perhaps best represented by Keith McGillivray's graphic impression of one of the sleek Irizar electric buses that Go-Ahead is likely to start running in south London in 2022.

A photo feature half a century ago used pictures from the *Belfast Telegraph* of corporation buses caught up in civil disorder as the Troubles unfolded in Northern Ireland. This year, Hugh Dougherty offers another insight into those times, with his graphic account of a day trip across the Irish border when his innocent pursuit of buses twice aroused the suspicion of security forces.

Two other contributors deserve special mention for their skills in restoring and enhancing some old photographs this year: Mike Eyre for most of those accompanying Roger Davies's look back to the 1960s and Peter Rowlands who, in addition to penning and illustrating an article of his own, has worked his magic on several in other articles.

I hope you enjoy all the contents of the pages that follow and that they live up to the high standard set half a century ago and maintained since then. ∎

Alan Millar

Cleaning the capital's air

With Transport for London aiming to have an entirely zero-emission bus fleet by 2030, **MARK LYONS** looks at the rapid rate at which it has stopped specifying diesel vehicles and recalls the previous generations of electric double-deckers that served many streets of the UK capital

One of the two BYD eBus battery-electric single-deckers with which Transport for London began the electrification of its network in 2013, Go-Ahead London General EB2 (LC63 CXY), at Waterloo. Pictures by MARK LYONS except where stated otherwise

Sadiq Khan, the mayor of London since 2016, wants London's buses to be zero tailpipe emission by 2030. These will be electric vehicles, deriving their power either from batteries or hydrogen fuel-cells.

Electric street transport is nothing new, but double-deck trams and trolleybuses are at best a memory for Londoners born before 1960 and a historical curiosity for the younger majority. The last of the first generation trams were withdrawn almost 70 years ago and the trolleybuses departed ten years later.

London's first electric trams ran in 1901 and upon its formation in 1933, the London Passenger Transport Board (better known as London Transport) acquired over 2,600 cars covering a network of nearly 350 route miles. The largest fleet taken over was that of London County Council.

It also inherited 61 trolleybuses, all operated by London United Tramways from Fulwell depot in south-west London. Their successful operation convinced the board that it should replace its remaining trams with trolleybuses, and between 1935 and 1940 the route network grew from 18 to 255miles while the tramways reduced to 102miles, mostly in south-east and south London.

The final tram to trolleybus conversion took place in June 1940, and the fleet had grown to over 1,700 vehicles by the time the last trolleybus ordered before the war was delivered in October 1941.

The decision to replace the remaining trams with motorbuses, rather than trolleybuses, was taken in 1946. The electrical equipment was nearing life expiry, diesel buses were cheaper to run and would operate flexibly without requiring the erection of overhead wires on the Embankment and Westminster Bridge. Objections to the apparent unsightliness of wiring at the heart of the capital was one reason why trolleybuses, like trams, had never penetrated the City or West End.

Operation Tramway, confirmed in March 1949, replaced trams with mainly new diesel buses in eight stages between October 1950 and July 1952.

Detailed plans to replace the trolleybuses with diesel buses were announced in April 1954 and implemented in 14 stages between March 1959 and May 8, 1962, with new 64-seat two-axle Routemasters replacing most of the three-axle 70-seaters. Most trolleybuses were scrapped, but a consortium of operators in Spain bought 125 of the 127 postwar Q1-class delivered in 1948 and 1952.

Trams return – not trolleybuses

Electric public transport was absent from London's streets for 38 years until May 2000 when the Croydon Tramlink opened. This is a modern light rail system rather than a street tramway like those replaced between 1935 and 1952. It uses articulated single-deckers and its 17 route miles are primarily on reserved track (some of it converted from heavy rail) with limited street running in central Croydon. There has been talk of extensions to Crystal Palace, Purley and Sutton, but none has yet proceeded.

There was talk of other tramways for London. The West London Tram between Shepherd's Bush and Uxbridge would have largely followed a tram route that subsequently became the 607 trolleybus, while the Cross River Tram would have linked Kings Cross and Camden with Peckham and Brixton.

Before the 2008 mayoral election, Labour's Ken Livingstone proposed an Oxford Street Tram linking Marble Arch and Tottenham Court Road as part of plans to pedestrianise Oxford Street.

The East London Transit, which is little more than a series of short bus priority measures in Barking Riverside, was conceived with a future upgrade to tramway, which has yet to materialise.

While Transport for London (TfL) and mayor Livingstone displayed brief enthusiasm for these tram projects, they exhibited little interest in trolleybuses. Artists' impressions of a proposed

The first generation of London Transport's electric street transport preserved at the East Anglia Transport Museum. Trolleybus 1201 (EXV 201) was new in 1939 with chassis and body built by Leyland. Tram 1858, with 74 seats, was built by London County Council in 1930. Parked between them is a 1936 AEC Mercury tower wagon used to provide maintenance staff with access to the overhead wires. TONY WILSON

Greenwich Waterfront Transit, intended to open in 2009, showed articulated single-deck trolleybuses on a segregated route connecting Abbey Wood, Thamesmead and Greenwich. Bus transit remains on the agenda, but not with trolleybuses.

In 2012, the car magazine *Autocar* floated the idea of double-deck trolleybuses, converted from New Routemasters, running along Oxford Street.

The zero-emission drive

One argument advanced by supporters of trams and trolleybuses is that they reduce urban air pollution. Road transport is a significant source of NOx, which forms NO2 in the atmosphere. Currently around 50% of NOx emissions in Greater London are from road transport, with buses making up about 20% of that 50%.

Although tram systems are being expanded in many cities around the world — including Birmingham, Edinburgh and Manchester in the UK — there is less enthusiasm for the trolleybus. The Moscow system, which following abandonment of London's network was the largest in the world, closed in August 2020. This followed the cessation

of trolleybus operation in Wellington, New Zealand in October 2017.

The last UK system, in Bradford, closed in 1972 and plans to reintroduce them to Leeds, as the rapid transit New Generation Transport network, were abandoned in 2016 after the Department for Transport ruled that they were not value for money.

Advances in battery and other technology make electric buses a realistic option without the infrastructure required for trolleybuses. The mayor of London's 2018 transport strategy envisaged that all new buses would be zero-emission from 2025, ready for an entirely zero-emission fleet by 2037.

TfL decreed that all new all new single-deckers delivered after October 2020 would be zero-emission. Although there is as yet no such commitment for double-deckers, no new diesel double-deckers have entered service on a TfL service since October 2020 and all outstanding

This extract from London Transport's 1947 tram and trolleybus map shows the limited extent to which electric street transport penetrated the central areas north of the River Thames. Solid red lines are trolleybus routes, broken lines are tram routes. Trams ran below street level between Bloomsbury and the Embankment.

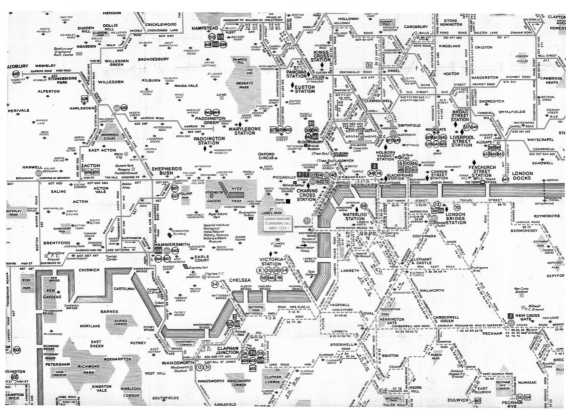

contract changes that require new vehicles specify zero-emission buses.

The aim now is to bring forward the target date to 2030. Of around 9,300 buses in London, approximately 700 will be zero-emission by the end of 2021, rising to 2,000 by 2025. An average of around 1,200 a year would be required to meet the target for 2030. The expiry dates of existing contacts mean that there are likely to be peaks in that requirement in 2023/24 and 2030/31. TfL may flatten or remove these peaks by introducing some new buses part way through a contract.

Hydrogen or battery?

All zero-emission buses have electric motors. What differentiates them is the source of that power.

Battery-electric buses are not new either. London's first mechanically-propelled bus, built by Radcliffe Ward, was trialled in 1889. Eight years later, the London Electric Omnibus Company demonstrated a similar vehicle, and in July 1907 the London Electrobus Company began running battery-powered buses between Victoria station and Liverpool Street.

They were popular with passengers and a second route was introduced between Victoria and Kilburn. However, the company ran into financial difficulties and ceased trading.in 1910.

Although electric road vehicles have been around for decades (think milk floats), their heavy lead acid cell batteries made them slow and limited in range.

Following operation with Metroline on route 98, five Chinese-built BYD double-deckers have gone to Uno for TfL schoolday services in north London. The large battery compartment over the rear wheels is apparent in this view of BYD1472 (LJ16 EZN) in Potters Bar.

Modern batteries are lighter, more compact and provide far greater range between charges.

TfL began to examine the potential for battery-electric buses in late 2011 and two 12m eBus single-deckers, built by Chinese manufacturer BYD, entered service with Go-Ahead London General in December 2013 on routes 507 (Waterloo-Victoria) and 521 (Waterloo-London Bridge).

BYD is primarily a manufacturer of batteries — including for mobile phones — and also is a volume builder of electric and hybrid cars. It claims to be the world's largest builder of electric vehicles.

The two BYDs were joined on the same routes in the summer of 2015 by two Irizar i2e single-deckers built in Spain. Although one of the two BYDs is now a museum piece, the Irizars have remained with Go-Ahead, operating from New Cross Garage on route 108 (Stratford-Lewisham).

Although these four vehicles were imported, TfL has also supported UK manufacturers' moves into the electric bus market, and in 2014 Optare supplied 13 battery-powered Metrocity lightweight single-deckers. Four went to RATP London United at Hounslow for route H98 (Hounslow-Hayes End) while the others were allocated to Arriva London South's Croydon garage for route 312 (Norwood

One of Abellio's e.City Gold single-deckers, 1532 (BV20 GUJ), meets a BYD/Alexander Dennis Enviro200EV in the RATP fleet, BE37017 (LJ18 FJZ), at Victoria.

Junction-South Croydon) where the four from Hounslow subsequently joined them.

BYD unveiled the K8SR, the first battery-electric double-decker for the UK, at Busworld Europe in Belgium in October 2015. Five were built in China for operation by Metroline in London, with the first of them launched in March 2016. They were allocated to Willesden garage and used alongside diesel buses on route 98 (Holborn-Willesden) until October 2019. They have since been used by Uno on schoolday TfL services in north London.

On single-deckers, batteries can be fitted on the roof, but that is impossible on a double-decker. These five have a large compartment at the rear, reducing the number of lower deck seats to 17, and total seating capacity to 54, two fewer than on a 1940s RT which was 7ft 6in shorter.

Production vehicles

Electrification moved beyond experimentation in August 2016, with start of the conversion of routes 507 and 521 to 100% battery operation.

By then, BYD had entered into a joint venture with Alexander Dennis that combined one of the world's biggest producers of electric buses with the UK's market leading bus builder. This gave the Chinese company quicker access to the UK and potentially other markets (starting with New Zealand) and accelerated the UK company's development of electric buses. Initially, BYD supplied chassis from China and later also from Hungary, but from 2021 Alexander Dennis integrated BYD driveline components into its own chassis built in the UK.

The buses for the conversion of the 507 and 521 were Enviro200EV single-deckers and many similar vehicles, of varying lengths, have since been delivered to other London operators. The Enviro200EV is by far the most common battery-electric single-decker in London, with 219 delivered to Go-Ahead, Metroline, RATP and Stagecoach by mid-2021 and more on order to fulfill contract awards.

Abellio London has purchased 34 Caetano e.City

Metroline-operated route 43 was the first double-deck route to go all-electric with 37 BYD/Alexander Dennis Enviro400EV City vehicles including BDE2617 (LJ19 CUC) crossing London Bridge.

Tower Transit OE34014 (YJ70 EVU), from the Australian-owned operator's order for 37 Optare Metrodecker EVs, in Park Lane.

Gold single-deckers for two routes operated from its Walworth garage. The Portuguese manufacturer plans to offer a double-deck variant.

Yutong E10 and Wright StreetAir battery-electric single-deckers have also been trialled by London operators, but no orders have yet been placed for either type. Yutong is the world's largest manufacturer of electric buses.

Production versions of battery-electric double-deckers were introduced from the summer of 2019 and the two types delivered then — the first 68 went to Metroline for two overlapping routes through north London — were still the only ones in London service two years later.

The BYD/Alexander Dennis Enviro400EV, with the City-style body influenced by the New Routemaster, is evolved from the design of the five BYD double-deckers trialled since 2016. Besides its British bodywork, a huge difference is that some of the batteries are under the floor ahead of the rear axle and behind the offside front wheel, enabling the standard 10.9m vehicle to have 24 lower deck seats in a two-door London layout and to have 43 upper deck seats instead of 37 in the prototypes.

The other double-decker is the Optare Metrodecker EV, built to a 10.5m length for London. This fully integral lightweight vehicle has 63 seats, 22 of them in the lower deck. Optare has renamed itself Switch Mobility and has adopted that brand name for its zero-emission buses.

Double-deckers in quantity

Metroline placed an initial order for 37 Enviro400EVs for operation from Holloway garage on route 43 (London Bridge-Friern Barnet) and 31 Metrodecker EVs for Potters Bar garage's route 134 (Warren St-North Finchley).

Subsequent contract awards specifying electric double-deckers had taken the total delivered to over 250 by mid-2021, with Metroline, RATP, Go-Ahead, Stagecoach and HCT Group having 184 Enviro400EVs, while besides Metroline's 31 Metrodeckers, Tower Transit had received most of its order for 37 of them and Go-Ahead had the first of 17 for a route that required shorter vehicles (a 10.3m Enviro400EV has since been added to the BYD/Alexander Dennis range). Optare's deliveries have been slower than Alexander Dennis's.

In June 2021, RATP London announced the biggest UK order so far for electric buses, for 68 Enviro200EVs and 127 Enviro400EVs.

Volvo (with MCV bodywork), Wrightbus, Caetano and Yutong have all announced plans to build battery-electric double-deckers for the UK, with London a key market.

The introduction of battery-electric buses requires the installation of charging equipment at garages which often calls for an upgrade to the power supply, while the space taken up by chargers can reduce parking space for buses. TfL's route tendering model means that an operator typically needs to have won an electric route contract before

An impression of the opportunity-charged Irizar ie Tram single-deckers that Go-Ahead London is likely to operate on south London suburban service 358 from 2022. KEITH MCGILLIVRAY

it can justify investing in such upgrades, and will undertake this on a route-by-route basis.

To accelerate the process, TfL is offering what it calls "grid-to-gate" grants to enable each garage to go all-electric in a single step.

Range anxiety

Although the energy density of batteries (the amount of power they can hold) has increased over recent years, the range of a battery electric bus is still only around 150miles on a single charge.

This is adequate for around 75% of London routes. For those where buses cover a greater distance in a day, one easy — but expensive — option is to have more buses and swap them over in the course of the day for recharging.

Another is opportunity charging, with batteries recharged in short bursts during the course of the day from a roadside gantry. This has already been adopted in the UK on Volvo 7900e single-deckers operated by The Harrogate Bus Company and Birmingham Airport. Go-Ahead London plans to install infrastructure at Bexleyheath garage to support the introduction of opportunity charged Enviro400EVs to route 132 (North Greenwich-Bexleyheath) in late 2021.

TfL also plans a bigger trial of opportunity charging on single-deck route 358 (Crystal Palace-Orpington) and has secured approval to install the necessary infrastructure at Orpington station and

Crystal Palace Parade. As with the equipment at Bexleyheath garage, a pantograph in each gantry will lower on to charging bars on the roof of the bus to deliver a quick blast of power.

The busy 358, run by Go-Ahead London's Metrobus operation, is 16miles from end to end and considered long by present day London standards. Buses cover over 170miles a day, which is beyond the range of current battery-electrics on a single charge. If the trial proceeds, Go-Ahead is likely to operate 20 rapid transit-styled 12m Irizar ie Tram single-deckers from early 2022.

Opportunity charging also reduces the battery capacity required, making this a possible solution for the small number of single-deck routes where particularly low bridges rule out the use of vehicles with large battery packs on their roofs.

Hydrogen power

Another answer to range anxiety is to use hydrogen fuel-cell buses, which use fuel-cells to convert the energy of hydrogen into electricity. They can run all day with a single fill of hydrogen. It takes several hours to fully charge a battery bus, but only a few minutes to refuel a hydrogen vehicle.

London's first fuel-cell buses were three Mercedes-Benz Citaros provided as part of the CUTE (Cleaner Urban Transport for Europe) programme. They ran for three years from January 2004, on part of route 25 (Oxford Circus-Stratford) before moving over to route RV1 (Tower Hill-Covent Garden) in September 2004. A refuelling facility was built at First London's Lea Interchange garage.

A more extensive trial followed in 2010 when five Wrightbus single-deckers with a Pulsar body built on a modified VDL SB200 chassis entered service on the RV1. Three similar vehicles followed in 2013 and were joined during 2018 by two Van Hool A330FC single-deckers funded through the CHIC (Clean Hydrogen in European Cities) project. All ten were withdrawn when the RV1 ceased in June 2019.

As with battery-electrics, TfL's goal has always been to have hydrogen fuel-cell double-deckers, and Wrightbus unveiled the world's first, a prototype StreetDeck H1, at a zero-emission bus summit in London in November 2016. The design was developed into the StreetDeck FCEV (for Fuel-Cell Electric Vehicle), 20 of which went into service with Metroline in 2021 on route 7 (Oxford Circus-East Acton), based at Perivale garage where hydrogen fuelling has been installed. These buses and supporting infrastructure were part funded by the European Union's JIVE (Joint Initiative for hydrogen Vehicles across Europe) project.

Alexander Dennis revealed details in February 2021 of the Enviro400 H2.0 City, powered by a Ballard fuel-cell power module and with a range of up to 300miles on a single fill. Switch is developing a fuel-cell version of the Metrodecker and Caetano demonstrated a single-deck H2.City Gold fuel-cell single-decker to Abellio London in October 2020.

Battery-electric buses are more expensive to buy than their diesel equivalents and hydrogen fuel-cell vehicles are significantly more expensive than battery-electrics. That said, the price of fuel-cell buses has decreased by more than 50% since the first generation, and is expected to fall as volume production enables the manufacture of their components in industrial quantities. Producing hydrogen is also highly energy intensive.

Although they produce no tail pipe emissions, the environmental credentials of battery-electric and fuel-cell vehicles depend on the composition of their batteries and the source of the energy they consume. Many automotive batteries require the mining of precious metals, and only if the energy is generated from a renewable source such as hydro, wind or tidal are they genuinely green.

Some things do not change. Over the 60 years when many Londoners relied upon trams and trolleybuses, the electricity that powered those zero-emission vehicles was generated in coal-fired power stations. ■

Metroline began operating its 20 hydrogen-fuelled Wright StreetDeck FCEV electric double-deckers, including WHD2711 (LK70 AZA), on route 7 in 2021. KRIS LAKE

Flying swords to passenger ploughshares

The end of hostilities in 1945 left many military aircraft engineering companies having to find new civilian outlets for their skills and services. **MIKE FENTON** tells the stories of three that ventured into bus and coach bodybuilding to meet a surge of demand as operators updated and enlarged their fleets with new vehicles.

In the aftermath of World War Two, and in order to find work for their employees, several companies that had been involved in manufacturing or repairing military aircraft diversified into building bus and coach bodies. One was the Lancashire Aircraft Corporation,

formed in July 1940. It had hangars at Samlesbury Airfield, at Balderstone between Blackburn and Preston, where it undertook aircraft repairs. With the end of the war in sight, talks were held in April 1945 between managing director Eric Rylands and Henry Spurrier, his counterpart at Leyland Motors,

with a view to Leyland subcontracting the building of some of its bus bodies.

Agreement was reached 12 months later for the construction, on an experimental basis, of a highbridge 56-seat double-deck body on a Titan PD1 chassis. After that, further examples followed in 1947, nine of which were supplied to Isle of Man Road Services on PD1A chassis, as shown by a black and white picture that Alan Cross took in 1951 of No.8 (GMN 778).

In addition to these, two on right-hand-drive PD1A chassis were supplied to the Companhia Carris de Ferro de Lisboa (Lisbon Electric Tramways), built with open platforms also on the right. One was CCFL 202 (HL-13-11), photographed in colour by Andrew Johnson in August 1963.

Not long after the delivery of the Lisbon buses, the Lancashire Aircraft Corporation set up a new limited company specifically for bodybuilding; this was Samlesbury Engineering, registered on May 16, 1947 and which continued to make subcontracted Leyland bodies for a time before branching out and producing bus and coach bodies of its own design. Besides Salmesbury, Leyland subcontracted the building of other bodies on PD1s to Alexander's Stirling coachworks in 1946/47.

Salmesbury Engineering also designed and built Bluebird K7, the jet-propelled hydroplane in which Donald Campbell set seven world water speed records between 1955 and 1964, and in which he was killed attempting to set an eighth in January 1967. The former Lancashire Aircraft Corporation site is still involved in aircraft manufacture, owned by BAE Systems.

Light alloy pioneer

The Scottish College of Aviation was registered in August 1935 as a training school for Royal Air Force pilots, with its base at Prestwick Aerodrome in south Ayrshire.

It was soon renamed Scottish Aviation and in 1939 began to manufacture components for Hawker Hurricane fighter aircraft. This was followed in 1940 by the construction of Westland Lysander aircraft, built in what had been the Palace of Engineering at the 1938 Empire Exhibition in Bellahouston Park, Glasgow, dismantled after the exhibition closed and re-erected at Prestwick.

Foden CCS 61 is described on p16.

With the ending of the war in 1945, the company engaged first in the conversion of Douglas C-47 Dakota aircraft for civilian use before moving on to the building of light alloy coach and double-deck bus bodies along aircraft principles.

During 1948, it built three 32-seat, full-fronted coach bodies on Foden chassis, one PVSC5 and two PVSC6. One of the latter pair was CCS 61, the fifth body the company built. This was first used as a demonstrator when registered in August 1948 and was sold after four months to Thomas Hunter of Kilmarnock, one of the members of the A1 Service cooperative, who kept it in his coach fleet until November 1965.

It then moved across the Firth of Clyde to the Isle of Arran, operating for around another five

years with Bannatyne's of Blackwaterfoot, a fleet based on the west of the island that also had three secondhand Albion Victors with Scottish Aviation bodies. The photograph of it on the previous page, from The Bus Archive, was by the late Harry Hay.

My second Scottish Aviation picture shows PS 2001, the only body it built on a Fordson ET6 chassis. This 29-seater was new in January 1951 to Ganson Bros. of Lerwick, Shetland. In 1964 it passed to RG Jamieson & Son of Cullivoe on the Shetland island of Yell, in whose ownership I photographed it in July 1973.

Production of bus and coach bodies at Prestwick ended in 1951, by which time a total of 131 had been produced. More than 80% of these were coaches, mainly on Commer and Albion chassis, with the balance made up mostly of 21 double-deck bus bodies. Twenty of these were supplied to Glasgow Corporation, five each on new Albion Venturer and Daimler CVD6 chassis, ten as rebodies of prewar AEC Regents. The other — the only one with a wide bonnet and concealed radiator — was on a Foden PVD6 chassis, registered JGD 675 in Glasgow in 1951 and operated for many years by Garelochhead Coach Services, with whom Iain MacGregor photographed it in 1965.

Two of Scottish Aviation's last bodies were single-deckers built on prototype underfloor-engined Albion KP71NW chassis with eight-cylinder horizontal engines, a dual-door bus for Glasgow

Corporation, BS1 (FYS 495), and an overnight coach for Western SMT, KI918 (BSD 470), which is understood to survive in preservation. Iain MacGregor photographed it at a vehicle gathering at Glasgow Airport in 1975.

One of the principal people behind Scottish Aviation's bodybuilding venture, William Howgate, moved to Alexander's coachbuilding business in 1948 as chief engineer and led its adoption of light alloy construction in bodies built from around 1950.

Scottish Aviation concentrated instead on aircraft manufacture and in 1977 became part of the then state-owned British Aerospace, which today is BAE Systems. It in turn sold the Prestwick business, which manufactures aircraft structures, in 2006 to United States-based Spirit AeroSystems along with a smaller operation coincidentally on the Salmesbury site.

Bristols from Portsmouth

Following a series of relocations and changes of name, the company that had started out as Flying Services — registered in April 1929 at Romford, Essex — settled at Portsmouth Airport, where in March 1943 it was renamed Portsmouth Aviation.

After undertaking aircraft maintenance and repairs during wartime, its prototype Aerocar Major five-seat light aircraft flew for the first time in June 1947, but plans for its production and that of other variants

were shelved after it attracted no buyers,.

By then the firm was rehabilitating passenger vehicle bodywork, after which it went on to build its own coach bodies, many of them for Hants & Dorset Motor Services on Bristol L chassis. In my eyes, the most elegant examples were 18 built in 1950 on L6G chassis as Hants & Dorset 667-84, as shown by this RHG Simpson view of 674 (KEL 402).

Coincidentally, the final Portsmouth Aviation-bodied vehicle also entered service in 1951, in the shape of Hants & Dorset Bristol LWL6G 781 (KLJ 751). It was, however, nowhere nearly as prolific as its Scottish counterpart, building just 37 bodies over a similar period of four years. ∎

Six wheels on my wagon

Operators' recent purchases of high-capacity tri-axle double-deckers have prompted **ALAN MILLAR** to look back over 90 years to consider other times when bus — and coach — fleets have concluded that four wheels just are not enough'

lsewhere in this *Yearbook,* Roger Davies and Robert Jowitt acknowledge the special appeal of buses with six wheels rather than four, three axles rather than two. For if a double-decker is deemed to be more of a bus — or coach — than a single-decker, then one with extra wheels has added presence.

Roger D suggests there is a snobbery among enthusiasts — and he pleads guilty to being one of them — who considered that, back in the day, a trolleybus system let itself down if it lacked a core fleet of high-capacity six-wheelers sweeping majestically through city streets.

There were six-wheel trolleys from Belfast to Newcastle, Glasgow to Nottingham, Manchester to Cardiff and points in between. Above all, they were abundant in London — by a huge margin the largest system in the country and then the largest in the world — where 1,890 of the 1,891 trolleybuses bought between 1931 and 1952 had six wheels. Most were 30ft long with 70 seats (ten of those downstairs

faced inwards over the rear wheels) and until 1956 regulations demanded an extra axle to bear the additional weight.

For the same reason, between 1929 and 1932 London General bought over 1,400 LT-class six-wheel motorbuses — single-deck and double — in far greater quantities than anyone did elsewhere. The Metropolitan Police stipulated a length of 27ft rather than 30ft for the double-deckers, but with their two-axle counterparts limited to 25ft and around 50 seats, a six-wheeler could hold ten more.

These used AEC's Renown chassis, the six-wheel equivalent of the Regent that was the basis of the General's ST class. While the Regent and its Regal single-deck equivalent had twin rear wheels, the Renown had single wheels on the rear axles. The drive on the Renown was distributed equally to both of those axles.

The six-wheel layout was abandoned as quickly as it had been adopted. It was heavy, scrubbed the rear tyres and increased fuel consumption. Once the permitted length limit of two-axle buses went up to 26ft, London could fit 60 seats into an STL-class two-axle Regent.

AEC sold relatively few Renowns outside London and Leyland fared no better with its six-wheel version of the Titan, the unfortunately named Titanic. Leyland met such demand as there was for 30ft single-deckers with a six-wheel Tiger.

The "Chinese Six"

These, and other manufacturers' six-wheelers, all had a similar layout with a single front steering axle and two drive axles at the rear. But in 1937 the Cheshire manufacturer ERF built what it claimed to be Britain's first lorry with two front steering axles and a single drive axle. This was a layout which for reasons possibly unfathomable came to be known as a "Chinese Six".

Leyland brought the same layout to a single-deck bus exhibited at the Commercial Motor Show in London that year. Not only did the Gnu have twin steering axles, but they were set back so the entrance — and engine — was on an overhang next to the driver. It built a solitary twin-steer trolleybus for London Transport (without the front overhang) in 1939 and a prototype Panda twin-steer single-decker with horizontal underfloor engine in 1940.

Apparent benefits were reduced tyre and brake wear, but war put paid to these promising ideas

and 20 years elapsed before a six-wheel passenger vehicle once again was available in the UK. This was the twin-steer Bedford VAL, which over ten years clocked up over 2,100 home and export sales.

Announced in September 1962 and produced until 1972, the front-engined VAL was Bedford's response to the legalisation of 36ft (11m) vehicles the previous year. Bus versions were built for North Western Road Car and British European Airways among others, and several others had van bodies, but the VAL was primarily a coach and Bedford's strength lay in producing lightweight, inexpensive vehicles for small, family-owned operators. The VAL fitted that mould. Three lighter axles instead of two heavier ones meant that the wheels could be smaller and the floor built lower.

The downside, which Bedford tried to alleviate, was more tyre and brake wear, and no other manufacturer chose this way of delivering longer vehicles. When Bedford replaced the VAL with its mid-engined YRT, the new model had four larger wheels and heavier axles.

Still, the VAL looked the part, a symbol of an optimistic age. The wheel arrangement combined with its length to look sleek and fast, especially on

Among the last six-wheel trolleybuses to be built was Huddersfield Corporation 631 (PVH 931), a 72-seat East Lancs-bodied Sunbeam S7 new in December 1959 and preserved at the Trolleybus Museum at Sandtoft.

Leyland only built eight twin-steer Gnus. This was the one exhibited at the 1937 Commercial Motor Show with 40-seat Alexander body incorporating front-end styling from America. It was one of two for Alexander's own fleet. LEYLAND

the growing motorway network. It was one of two contemporary buses and coaches that Dinky Toys modelled for the mass market in the 1960s; the other was Leyland's revolutionary rear-engined Atlantean double-decker.

The VAL influenced other engineers seeking to lower bus floors and reduce wheelbox intrusion into seating space. Those at Leyland developing what became the Leyland National completed a mock-up in 1967 called Commutabus which possessed much of the look of the vehicle put into production four years later but had not just six, but eight small wheels, two for steering.

Besides the concerns about tyre and brake wear and technical complexity, what it gained in reduced floor height was compromised by the seats over the wheels having to face inwards. The Leyland National had a conventional four-wheel arrangement.

London Transport engineers, working from the early 1970s on an ultimately abandoned project to design a bespoke double-decker codenamed XRM, conceived it as having eight small wheels and a side engine, and might also have incorporated a revolutionary hydraulic drive system. They acquired a secondhand VAL to test out their ideas, but the project evolved into a shorter bus with larger wheels before being abandoned in the 1980s.

Bigger for the 1980s

British manufacturers had built six-wheel double-deckers over the years for export customers and by the early 1980s this business was gaining momentum in Hong Kong where capacity of the bus service was increased through the use of large

Stagecoach has preserved 14000 (F110 NES), the 1988 Megadekka, a 110-seat Alexander RL-bodied Leyland Olympian, in its heritage collection.

Two of Stagecoach Manchester's Duple Metsec-bodied Dennis Dragons in Hathersage Road on a Magic Bus service in 2010. They retained the deep sliding windows from their first use in Kenya. JOHN YOUNG

double-deckers developed from those they built for UK customers.

MCW and Leyland produced longer tri-axle versions of their Metrobus and Olympian chassis, Volvo produced a few similarly configured front-engine Ailsas and Dennis created a three-axle Dominator called either Dragon or Condor depending on which Hong Kong customer bought it. All were single-steered and on the rear-engined models only the rearmost axle was driven, while the one directly ahead was steered to improve manoeuvrability.

There nearly was a twin-steer version too. The truck builder Fodens, which had dabbled with buses and coaches before, offered a front-engined chassis for Hong Kong — a "Chinese Six" for a territory in China — but the manufacturer went into receivership in 1980 before it could be produced and its new American owner, Paccar, had no interest in buses.

Deregulation of domestic express coach services, and expansion of coach travel into mainland Europe, generated demand for 12m tri-axle vehicles, many of them double-deck. Besides being able to carry more passengers, the extra axle helped accommodate their luggage and the hefty boxes of beer, wine and other duty free purchases that international travellers were likely to make.

The tri-axle double-deck coaches included established models like the Neoplan Skyliner from Germany and Van Hool Astromega from Belgium. There also was a home-grown offer bought mainly by the state-owned National Bus Company and Scottish Bus Group. The 12m MCW Metroliner, with a Cummins engine, was developed from the tri-axle Metrobus for Hong Kong and styled as a coach. As a full-height vehicle, it offered better headroom for passengers than on the 4m high continental imports, but that restricted it to UK roads.

MCW built 151 between 1982 and 1987, and also three 4m high Metroliner 400GTs before closing down. Plaxton developed its first ever double-deck coach, the Paramount 4000, in 1984 and built 99 on tri-axle Neoplan, Scania, DAF and Volvo chassis.

At the other end of the scale, the industry's embracing of minibuses from the mid-1980s included small numbers of tri-axle low-floor Talbot Express and CVE Omni vehicles. These were outliers in a class of vehicle which generally was as mechanically uncomplicated as possible.

Olympians from Hong Kong

The swing to high-frequency minibuses was driven by the deregulation of local bus services and privatisation of most of the public sector operators that provided them. These service providers were open to other ideas and Stagecoach, starting to build up a business from privatised NBC subsidiaries, was the first to buy tri-axle double-deckers for bus routes.

Wellglade Group's TM Travel has bought two of the East Lancs Nordic-bodied Volvo B7Ls new to First Glasgow in 2002. This one was demonstrating its manoeuvrability on the Chatsworth estate in Derbyshire. TONY WILSON

It already preferred longer two-axle vehicles to shorter ones and in early 1988 supplemented its orders for 87-seat lowheight Alexander-bodied Leyland Olympians with three based on the 12m tri-axle chassis built for Hong Kong. Two for routes serving the Sellafield nuclear site in Cumbria had 96 seats while the other, branded Megadekka and "Britain's Biggest Bus", was a 110-seater operated initially in Glasgow.

The trio remained unique, but Stagecoach bought 20 tri-axle Dennis Dragons in 1995/96 for a business it then owned in Kenya, where their Duple Metsec bodies were assembled, and shipped them to Manchester four years later, operating them as 88-seaters on low-fare Magic Bus routes.

Many more tri-axle double-deckers followed, one way or another as a consequence of two of the big groups' involvement in Hong Kong, the home of so many six-wheelers.

From 1998 to 2000, FirstGroup held a minority shareholding in and provided the operational expertise for New World First Bus, a new company awarded franchises for routes provided until then by China Motor Bus. From 1999 to 2003, Stagecoach owned Citybus, another of the former UK territory's major operators. Together with Hong Kong's largest bus company, Kowloon Motor Bus (KMB), they replaced many older tri-axle double-deckers with air-conditioned new ones.

As they exited Hong Kong, they repatriated surplus double-deckers to their UK fleets. First brought ten 11m Alexander-bodied Leyland Olympians from New World. The standard body arrangement in Hong Kong was to have a narrow front entrance and full-width centre exit, and these vehicles, built in 1993, had 109 seats squeezed in partly a 3+2 configuration. First rebuilt them with a full-width front door and 84 seats, a significant proportion of those on the lower saloon facing inwards as on a London tube train. These vehicles migrated from Greater Manchester to Glasgow and on to East Anglia.

Stagecoach brought 54 Alexander-bodied 12m Olympians from Citybus, all single-door 94-seaters, and purchased 21 two-door vehicles from KMB and rebuilt them with one door and 118 seats; the Citybus vehicles had Cummins engines, while those from KMB a Gardner 6LXCT. Many were for Magic Bus in Manchester, but some of the coach-seated ex-Citybus vehicles — and some of the Dragons from Kenya — helped launch Megabus longer distance services in 2003. Stagecoach later used some of the Olympians as rail replacement vehicles on lines where the group held train operating franchises, also as high-capacity schoolbuses.

Many other surplus Hong Kong buses were

imported by dealers who saw the potential for Metrobuses, Olympians, Dragons and Condors either as schoolbuses or open-top sightseeing vehicles.

Nordics and Enviro500s

The Hong Kong connection also brought new tri-axle double-deckers to UK bus services from 2002. One of First's managers, Mark Savelli, returned to Britain after the group sold its shareholding in New World First Bus to head its operation in Glasgow where low-floor 40-seat single-deckers had replaced many double-deckers. Convinced that it could attract more passengers if they could secure a seat, he persuaded the group not just to buy double-deckers, but big ones with three axles and air conditioning.

East Lancs had already won orders from Copenhagen for lowheight bodies with three doors and two staircases on a tri-axle 12m low-floor Volvo B7L chassis, a design the Blackburn coachbuilder called the Nordic. It was best placed to meet Savelli's dream with a right-hand-drive single-door, single-staircase version with 95 seats. First leased ten of them.

Savelli moved on to another job and no more were ordered, although East Lancs and Volvo built open-top versions for continental Europe. After around ten years, First returned the Glasgow buses to Volvo and most moved on to the Brightbus company in South Yorkshire, operating alongside several ex-Hong Kong six-wheelers on schools services.

That was not the end of the story of Savelli or six-wheelers. He returned to head First's Scottish operations and once again persuaded the group to buy air-conditioned, low-floor, six-wheel double-deckers for Glasgow, which were delivered in 2009. These were more like contemporary machines in Hong Kong, 25 Alexander Dennis Enviro500s with 82 seats. The Cummins-engined Enviro500 was based on the tri-axle Trident that Dennis developed for the Far East in 1997.

These were the first and only Enviro500s for the home market. The air conditioning contributed towards poor fuel consumption and they were transferred to a busy cross-city route in Aberdeen, with the aircon replaced by opening windows.

They are not the only Enviro500s built for the British Isles, however, as Dublin Bus bought 20 on tri-axle Volvo B9TL chassis in 2005 and 50 more in 2007, all with 91 seats. The first 20 have since been sold, most to UK operators for school transport and rail replacement work.

East Lancs was able to exploit a niche market for new tri-axle private hire and open-top sightseeing double-deckers mainly from operators looking to replace secondhand examples from Hong Kong. It built both the Nordic and its Olympus successor

First Aberdeen operates its 25 Alexander Dennis Enviro500s mainly on the "Bridges" routes linking the Bridge of Don to the north with Bridge of Dee to the south, replacements for the city's last tram service in 1958. PHIL HOWARD

One of Stagecoach's tri-axle Scania OmniLinks on hire to Reading Buses for its Green Line service between London and Windsor in early 2018. MARK LYONS

(the latter called Visionaire when open-top) on B9TL chassis, typically with around 100 seats and some coach features, until new owner Optare closed the Blackburn factory in 2011.

The last 16 were 97-seat 12.3m Visionaires for the Original London Sightseeing Tour, then owned by Arriva. Big Bus Company bought six similar vehicles in 2010 and supplemented them in 2012 — the year of the London Olympics — with 20 tri-axle open-toppers built by Ankai in China.

Stagecoach's enthusiasm for tri-axle vehicles was not confined to double-deckers or local service buses. It took advantage of the increase in permitted lengths to 15m to buy high-capacity coaches, particularly for the Megabus fleet, and in 2007 bought nine 13.7m six-wheel Scania OmniLink 56-seat single-deck buses for commuter services between Fife and Edinburgh across the Forth Road Bridge, which is often closed to high-sided vehicles in strong winds. Scania sold similar vehicles to a few other operators.

Most of the Scanias have since gone, but their place on the Fife-Edinburgh routes was taken by 19 tri-axle 14.6m Volvo B8RLEs with 53-seat low-floor Plaxton Panther LE bodies delivered in 2018. This was a design commissioned by Stagecoach, which at the time of writing was still the only customer. It also was the launch customer for Plaxton's Panorama double-deck coach launched concurrently on Volvo's tri-axle B11RLE chassis.

Stagecoach and First between them operated ten tri-axle Van Hool A330 hydrogen fuel-cell single-deckers delivered in 2014 for a trial, since ended, in Aberdeen.

Edinburgh beats London

Besides the sightseeing fleets, London — once home of around 3,000 six-wheelers on ordinary public service — resisted attempts to buy their modern successors for red bus routes. In the 1990s, Capital Citybus — owned then by Citybus in Hong Kong — tried to persuade London Transport to let it operate tri-axle Olympians and demonstrated a new one for Hong Kong to prove its point.

There were fresh suggestions a decade or so later that 12m tri-axle double-deckers were a more suitable means of handling growing traffic than 18m articulated bendybuses, but Transport for London — as the authority was now called — remained unconvinced.

That was until 2018 when Ensignbus provided Go-Ahead London with the bus on the cover of this book, a Chinese-built 12.5m tri-axle BCI hybrid with a 78-seat two-door body, for trial on route 12 through south-east London. It remains the only tri-axle double-decker on the network and was the first since the trolleybus system closed in 1962.

Spotting a gap in the market left when Optare closed the East Lancs factory, Ensignbus began importing straight diesel BCI tri-axle double-deckers two years earlier and put eight with 98 seats into its own fleet, mainly for private hires and rail replacement work, and sold another to Aintree Coachline on Merseyside. Most have Cummins engines, but the newest in the Ensignbus fleet has a Chinese-made Weichai unit.

It would take another of the UK's capital cities — Edinburgh — to embrace tri-axle double-deckers. Lothian Buses' principal chassis supplier was Volvo,

which in 2017 had replaced the transverse-engined B9TL with a new tri-axle chassis for Hong Kong and Singapore, the B8L with Euro6 emissions compliant engine mounted inline. The chassis, with front frame modified, became available in the UK the following year.

It was offered with bodywork by Wrightbus, which built most of the first vehicles ordered for Hong Kong, Egyptian coachbuilder MCV which was rapidly becoming Volvo's main body partner for the UK, and by Alexander Dennis which had supplanted Wrightbus as Lothian's preferred body supplier.

MCV built eight 80-seat closed-top EvoSeti bodies on 12m B8Ls delivered to Golden Tours in 2020, primarily to shuttle visitors between central London and the Harry Potter film studios in Hertfordshire. All other B8Ls to date have dual-door Alexander Dennis bodies on a longer — 13.4m (43ft) — chassis.

Lothian, led by its then managing director Richard Hall, wanted a two-door bus with 100 seats and worked closely with Alexander Dennis on a lengthened version of its Enviro400 body, branded Enviro400XLB. It put 78 into service in 2019, of

Fifteen of Lothian's Alexander Dennis Enviro400XLB-bodied Volvo B8Ls were built for its Airlink airport service, with smoked glass, reduced seating and extra luggage racks.
KEITH MCGILLIVRAY

which 15 for its airport service have 81 seats and additional luggage racks.

Stagecoach bought 12 similar vehicles in 2019, its first new tri-axle double-deck buses (rather than coaches) for the UK since the 1988 Olympians, for the Cambridgeshire guided busway; these have 98 seats, leaving additional space for passengers with baby buggies.

Is this a new dawn for tri-axle buses or another false one? Lothian has since bought more two-axle Volvo B5TLs with one-door Enviro400 bodies, but maybe has all the 100-seaters it requires for now. The Covid-19 pandemic has cast doubt over what level of demand there will be for public transport when normal life returns and whether such huge vehicles are needed.

If there are to be more, then they will surely share one essential feature of the tri-axle double-deckers that served London from 1931 to 1962 — and many other places over a similar timespan — by being powered by electricity. ■

Photo finish

8 4 WIBSEY

75

HKW 75

This gloomy 1952 AEC photo features a Bradford Corporation Regent III sporting a "new-look" front of a style normally associated with Daimler and Guy. One of 40, the body was by East Lancs.

GAVIN BOOTH shares some examples of his collection of manufacturers' official photographs and divulges a few tricks of the publicity trade that have been deployed to make some of them appear to be more authentic than they actually are

It was sometime in the late 1950s when I first realised that bus builders arranged for proper photographs to be taken of their products. And it soon became clear that some operators also used local photographers to record what they were doing.

As a spotty teenager, my mission was to get hold of some of these photos, particularly of buses that operated around my home city of Edinburgh. So I found the addresses of the companies that built my local buses and posted off handwritten letters asking for prints.

Needless to say, most of these letters probably ended up filed in the wastepaper bin, but some manufacturers, bless them, sent glossy black-and-white prints, probably in the hope that this would deter me from ever writing again. Eastern Coach Works and Metro-Cammell, as I recall, came up with the goods but my collection remained fairly small until I started going to bus shows and hung around looking pathetic, mopping up brochures

and occasional photo prints from the stands.

Most manufacturers produced record shots, as much for their own archives as for sending out to

The Leyland photographer must have been allowed out to photograph this Leigh Corporation Titan PD2/20 with lowbridge East Lancs body in 1956, complete with what look like real passengers.

Saunders built 250 bodies for London Transport RT-class AEC Regent IIIs between 1949 and 1951 in its factory at Beaumaris on Anglesey. A line of these pauses for the Saunders photographer on the Menai Bridge linking Anglesey with mainland Wales in 1950 as they started their 290mile drive to London.

Preston's then seven-year-old iconic bus station stood in for downtown Manhattan in this Leyland photograph of one of eight Atlanteans with air-conditioned Park Royal bodies built in 1976 for operation in New York City. Their left-hand-drive chassis was to similar to large numbers Leyland built then for Teheran.

Members of the office staff from the Alexander coachworks pretend to be passengers at a bus stop in the main road immediately opposite the factory. The undersized "Glasgow" destination had been borrowed from a Scottish Omnibuses AEC Reliance coach. The bus is a 1960 Glasgow Corporation Leyland Titan PD3/2, so at least the photo was taken in Glasgow Road.

BELOW: *AEC built the chassis, so there are fewer photos of completed buses outside the Southall works featuring the prominent AEC logo, but this 1956 Rochdale Corporation Regent V, with Gardner 6LW engine, was bodied by Weymann at Addlestone, also in the London area, so could drop in on its way north to Lancashire.*

the trade press to publicise their latest deliveries. Bodybuilders used local professional photographers to take what were simply record shots – a bus, paint barely dry, driven out to a quiet corner of the yard for photography, typically a three-quarter front and nearside shot, with destination blinds set randomly and inevitably inaccurately – particularly if they could find a humorous destination while winding through. Sometimes this would be the first bus of a batch, sometimes the last as somebody realised they needed a record shot before it was driven off to its customer.

These shots, though often pretty soulless, provide historians with an invaluable, good quality record of how buses looked when they were straight out of the box before operators started to modify the specification or apply different livery styles. For preservationists taking a bus back to its as-delivered state, they are a godsend.

Classic street scenes

Chassis builders would usually have technical photos taken for their own use, but often only circulated their official photos to the transport press when a new model was introduced. Although they rarely saw their products in their bodied, passenger-ready state, the more enterprising ones arranged for in-service photos to be taken of bus deliveries they were particularly proud of. AEC and Leyland were good at this and the results include some stunning period street scenes of buses carrying real passengers.

The most comprehensive collection of official photos must be London Transport's. Right from the early days of London General and into the London Transport era, the value of a photographic record was embraced enthusiastically, so every aspect of the business was recorded, giving us access to a treasure trove of splendid images, including amazing street scenes.

Leyland had an in-house photographic department from its earliest days, building up a wonderful collection of images. In 1975, I was fortunate to have access to this when I was marketing manager at the Scottish Bus Group and the 70th anniversary of the group's inception was coming up in 1976.

I spent two fascinating days at Leyland poring

Roe-bodied buses were often photographed outside the office block at its Leeds factory, ensuring the logo above the door was included. This is a Teesside Leyland Atlantean PDR1/3 for Teesside Municipal Transport.

Twenty-five Plaxton Pointer-bodied Dennis Dart SLFs, for London Transport services operated by Armchair neatly fill the garage parking area in 1997 after considerable shunting. They even appear to be in registration number order.

Confusing enthusiasts in 1996, but looking more convincing than a blank panel, this Wright Crusader-bodied Dennis Dart SLF of Universitybus (the first with a Floline ramped floor) carries the temporary dateless identity a long scrapped 1960 Leyland Atlantean, XVA 444, for the purposes of photography.

through immaculately handwritten ledgers dating back even farther than SBG and listing all the photos taken. This allowed me to identify photos of buses of SBG and its constituents, and Leyland looked out the glass plate negatives and bravely sent them up to Edinburgh where I arranged for prints to be made before I returned them, very carefully packed. I do not imagine Leyland was normally so accommodating with its precious negatives, but then again SBG was buying new Leylands by the hundred.

Later, in the 1990s, after SBG companies were privatised, I was freelancing for any transport publications that would give me work and as a consequence received press releases and photos from several major bus builders. By this time, photos were usually colour prints and while some were record shots, others showed buses in service – or apparently in service – and these certainly had more life to them.

My good friend Stewart Brown took many of these, the advantage of being both a good photographer and someone with an interest in, and knowledge of buses. You sometimes felt that images taken by the local photographic studio lacked imagination because it was just a job, crammed in between a presentation by the local mayor, a dog show or the local works dinner dance.

Stewart recalls that he would arrange to visit the company that had just received new products – often from Dennis or Plaxton, or indeed both. Sometimes he would arrive to find that the bus was in service and, armed with its schedule, he would suss out a good vantage point and wait for it.

Uncertain weather

Other times he would have the bus and driver to himself, to go out looking for suitable spots for photography, hoping that he could at least make it look as if it was in service. The only uncertainty was often the British weather, so dark, wet days were inevitable, but with a friendly operator and a bit of patience a satisfactory result was usually possible.

I did some photographic work for the Walter Alexander coachworks at Falkirk in the 1990s and can understand the frustrations involved when trying to get good photos of a new bus. Sometimes the bus wasn't available, or could only be spared for

A slightly squashed version of the 1960 prototype Daimler Fleetline, 7000 HP, released before the finished Weymann-bodied bus was ready for photography. At least Daimler's artist got the registration right. Compare it with the real thing and it was a decent likeness.

an hour or so because it was due to be shown to the customer or delivered or collected.

If time was short, the bus was parked in front of the giant WA logo on the main front wall of the factory. If there was a bit more time and a company driver was available, we quickly got to know the places around Falkirk where you could photograph a bus in vaguely appropriate surroundings and in the right light without causing major traffic disruption.

Before Alexander moved its coachbuilding

Alexander released the fanciful "Artist's Pre-release Impression" of its new P-type bus, which was never going to win prizes for its looks, although the real thing was better proportioned, represented here by a preserved Northern Scottish Dennis Lancet new in 1984.

activities to Falkirk in 1958 the business was based in Stirling, which had the advantage of an impressive castle not far from the Drip Road factory. Falkirk is a bit lacking in the castle department, though in recent years it has had the

WALTER ALEXANDER'S NEW RANGE OF STAGE-CARRIAGE BUSES

Artist's Pre-release Impression
The new 'P' type Service Bus. Available for 1983 delivery.

Robust Light Aluminium Alloy structure with a design and specification honed and tailored to meet the operators requirements for the eighties.

This vividly colourful photo from 1995 shows a Wright Endurance-bodied Volvo B10B for GM Buses North outside Manchester's G-Mex Centre. Note that the operator's livery draws attention to the "low floor", although this was a step-entrance vehicle with a low-ish floor, rather than the fully-accessible step-free variety already available.

advantage of the backdrop of the amazing Falkirk Wheel, the boat lift that joins two sections of canal.

Roe was another coachbuilder making use of the company logo on the front of its Leeds offices by ensuring that many of its official photos were taken to include this.

The Good, the Bad and the Ugly

Looking through my collection of official photos to find some to share with you in these pages, I realise there are some that are very good, others not so good, some that are, in retrospect, weird, and some that today just seem funny. The Good, the Bad and the Ugly, in fact.

The Good tend to be the in-service photos taken

The picture on the left was the photo released by Leyland before its lowheight Albion Lowlander was launched – or even ready – in 1961. The offside photo reveals that little more of the bus actually existed at this stage.

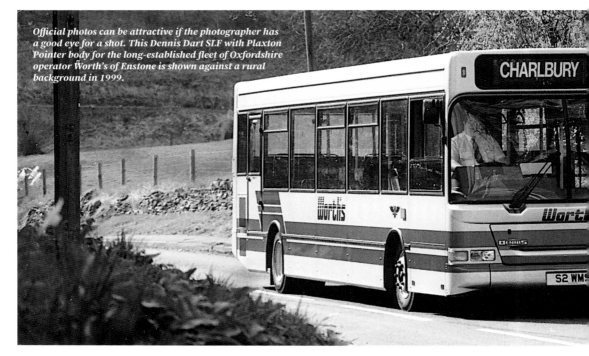

Official photos can be attractive if the photographer has a good eye for a shot. This Dennis Dart SLF with Plaxton Pointer body for the long-established fleet of Oxfordshire operator Worth's of Enstone is shown against a rural background in 1999.

by and for the likes of AEC and Leyland, and more recently for Dennis and Plaxton. AEC's photographers would occasionally take photos at the company's spiritual home at Southall, in west London, but that was purely a chassis plant so there were relatively few complete buses hanging around. So they were despatched to find AEC buses in service, or briefed a local photographer to seek them out. The end result was a series of fine in-service shots that included period cars, people, shopfronts – often views that have long since gone.

Arch-rival Leyland did this to an extent. When it was building complete buses – from the earliest days through to 1954 and then from the Leyland National era onwards to Leyland's sad demise – these were photographed routinely. But Leyland too had to record buses with bodies built elsewhere and some fine in-service views remind us of these times.

Even in the years before 1954, you got the feeling that its photographers were permitted the odd away day – but not too many of them and not too far away. Ribble, on Leyland's doorstep, and the Lancashire municipalities feature in many fine views that do not try to distort reality with buses posed against inappropriate backgrounds like stately homes, prominent monuments or public parks. The legacy is a selection of quality images that capture the sometimes gritty reality of 1950s Lancashire.

Necessary illusions

Bodybuilders had the advantage that they had complete buses to capture on camera and in addition to the stock views against familiar backgrounds close to – even around – the factory, there were some notable exceptions.

In 1960, Alexander posed a Glasgow Corporation Leyland Titan PD3 at the bus stop opposite its factory in Glasgow Road, Falkirk, found a destination blind with "Glasgow" on it and wheeled most of its office staff out to pretend to be passengers.

When people were included – real or pretend passengers – photographers seemed to prefer that someone should be standing at the entrance with one foot on the step and the other holding a grabrail, often looking at the camera, which destroyed the illusion. Another ploy with pretend passengers on board was to ask them to sit only by the windows on the side that was being photographed to make the bus look busy.

Manufacturers and operators often liked photos with not just one but a line of new buses to brag about the size of their investment.

This can work, but often required a great deal of space and a great deal of manoeuvring to get the buses into line, particularly if somebody wanted them in fleetnumber order. Photos like this can be

effective, but can also simply show a long line of buses disappearing into the sunset.

False identity

When photographing a single brand-new bus, there are a few points that are worth getting right. If the bus got there on trade plates, then hide them. If it's unregistered, rustle up a believable registration plate, though this can confuse historians in future years if it is incorrect.

When *Buses Yearbook* editor Alan Millar was doing some photographic work for Wrights and Arriva Bus & Coach in the 1990s, he carried a false dateless plate in his car; it was for a bus that had long since gone to the great scrapyard in the sky – XVA 444, an early Leyland Atlantean that had been delivered to the Scottish independent Laurie of Hamilton. While these looked right when temporarily applied to a new bus or coach, it led to many conspiracy theories among the enthusiast fraternity and was only used twice.

And what do you do if you have a press release ready to send out about a new model, but the first example isn't ready? Manufacturers have tried various solutions. You can put out an artist's impression to whet the appetite, though some look as if the artist hasn't seen the accurate drawings, or perhaps even a bus. Or you can doctor a picture of a vaguely similar bus and hope nobody notices.

Or, most impressively, you can build the front part of a bus and photograph it so that nobody notices that three-quarters of the bus is actually missing. Leyland did this with the first Albion Lowlander – convincing until you see how much bus there actually was. Or wasn't.

Unintended consequences

And there is the Law of Unintended Consequences. The photographer has finished with the bus itself and the client wants VIPs included in the photo. This can be as simple as handing over the keys – sometimes convenient car keys – to the customer, but if the photographer is looking for an arty shot he might position the VIPs in a more novel setting.

Like the Alexander photo shown below, taken at the handover of a Lothian Volvo Olympian and featuring senior staff from Alexander, Lothian and Volvo who, standing behind high grasses, were presumably told to look purposefully into the distance with the bus in the background. The result, as you can see, was more than slightly ludicrous – but at least the buses performed well.

Sadly for my collection, the days of glossy hand-out prints are over. Sure, we get emailed images, we got CDs for a while, and now memory sticks – all very efficient and 21st century. But where's the joy in collecting these? ∎

Senior bus industry figures looking slightly uncomfortable as they gaze into the distance in front of a 1996 Alexander Royale-bodied Volvo Olympian Lothian. Those in the awkward line-up are, from the left, Bill Cameron CEO Alexander, Charles Evans CEO Lothian, Sandy Glennie MD Volvo Bus and Anthony Pursey, also from Alexander.

First Hampshire & Dorset 32329 (620 HOD), an open-top Wright Eclipse Gemini-bodied Volvo B7TL in Jurassic Coaster livery, at the Durdle Door on the Dorset coast in June 2021 on the newly introduced X52 service linking the Monkey Sanctuary at Wool, east of Weymouth, with Bridport to the north-west. This bus was originally a two-door vehicle with First London, numbered VNZ32329 (LK53 LYJ).

Staycation specials

With domestic holidays expected to be more popular than trips abroad, major operators in south-west England increased their open-top and other tourist services for the summer of 2021. **RICHARD GODFREY** captured some of the variety as the season began

BELOW: First South West's new services included an open-top sightseeing tour of Exeter for which Plaxton President-bodied Dennis Trident 32727 (V527 ESC) came from First's Bright Bus Tours fleet in Edinburgh. It was photographed at Exeter Quay. This bus was new to Lothian Buses in 1999 and saw subsequent service with West Coast Motors before First acquired it in 2019.

The trunk Jurassic Coaster X53 service connects Axminster with Weymouth. Passing through the village of Abbotsbury, famed for its swannery (hence the name on the pub sign) in March 2021 was First Hampshire & Dorset 33707 (SN12 AHU), an Alexander Dennis Enviro400 from a fleet of 100 purchased to operate at the London Olympics in 2012.

A previous open-top sightseeing venture in Exeter, also photographed at the Quay, was in 1994 when independent operator Red Bus Services used VDV 818, an AEC Regent V new to Devon General in 1957. Its Metro-Cammell Orion body was converted in 1973.

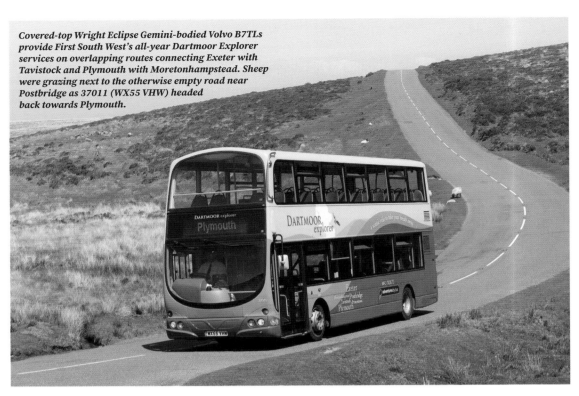

Covered-top Wright Eclipse Gemini-bodied Volvo B7TLs provide First South West's all-year Dartmoor Explorer services on overlapping routes connecting Exeter with Tavistock and Plymouth with Moretonhampstead. Sheep were grazing next to the otherwise empty road near Postbridge as 37011 (WX55 VHW) headed back towards Plymouth.

First Hampshire & Dorset's open-top Portland Coaster service links Weymouth with Portland Bill. Alexander ALX400-bodied Volvo B7TL 32031 (OIG 6947), passing through Portland Heights, is one of three similar vehicles originally operated on Southampton city services.

First South West purchased two open-top Scania OmniCity double-deckers from Lothian's East Coast Buses fleet to operate its new Exmoor Coaster service between Lynmouth and Minehead. The spectacular coastline stretches out behind 36801 (SN57 DBY) as it climbs Countisbury Hill on the A39 out of Lynmouth.

Stagecoach South West converted three Alexander Dennis Enviro400s, including 19107 (MX07 HMG), to open-top for The Wave-branded service 21C between Branstaple and Croyde Bay in north Devon. They are painted in a variation of the group's local service livery.

Orange-liveried Line 1 ran parallel to the coastal tramway to cater for free concessionary pass holders from more distant parts of England, and was operated by double-deckers that were also used on schools work. In September 2010, these included East Lancs-bodied Leyland Olympian 368 (F368 AFR) which had previously worn Line 11 turquoise. It was photographed passing Queen's Terrace in Fleetwood at the start of its journey south to Starr Gate.

Metro Coastlines

MARK BAILEY recalls a colourful period when Blackpool Transport identified each of its main routes with a unique identity

At the start of the present millennium, Blackpool Transport engaged the TAS Consultancy to study the usage patterns across its network of routes and recommend ways of revitalising ridership by the resident population of Blackpool, Fleetwood and Lytham St Annes.

Having established what routes it would run, it then commissioned Ray Stenning and his team at Best Impressions to create a cohesive new brand to help it implement these changes.

It rebranded its operations as Metro Coastlines on April 30, 2001. This was effectively a tweaking of the existing routes (now called lines) but with higher frequencies, and each line distinguished by its own unique colour.

On the vehicles, the individual line colour was complemented by yellow relief across most of the fleet. In time, this replaced the traditional network-wide livery of cream and green, except on Leyland Atlanteans, the last of which were kept until 2009,

and none of which received the new colours.

Blackpool Transport paid considerable attention to ensuring that buses ran on their correct lines and a few were painted in a "pool" livery of grey, yellow and mustard, capable of filling in as and when required. Several others sported an all-routes black and yellow livery, similar to that worn previously by its HandyBus minibus fleet.

The single-route tramway (line T) was not given a specific new livery, but several trams were repainted in a variety of the new colours. Many others retained overall advertising liveries, as this was an important revenue stream.

The new brand and individual colours lasted for eight years. A decision was taken in late 2009 to discontinue the Metro Coastlines branding, heralding the end of this fascinating and colourful episode. Subsequent additions to the bus fleet were painted in a revamped black and yellow standard livery, superseded today by grey and lemon with Palladium branding. ■

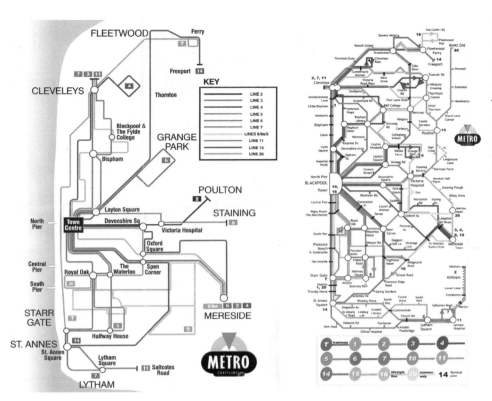

The Metro Coastlines network was altered from its original format, as these maps from 2001 and 2008 show, with routes 1, 10, 15, 16 and 20 added, and 8/8a, 9 and 26 replaced.

One of the first vehicles repainted into a Metro Coastlines livery was Optare Delta-bodied DAF SB220 115 (H115 YHG), which wore the claret Line 6 scheme. It was photographed in August 2001 loading outside the town centre BHS department store in Church Street, which closed in August 2016. The bus had come from Grange Park and was heading on to Mereside.

In 2002, Line 26 was merged into Line 2, which assumed its light green livery. Optare MetroRider 506 (S506 LHG) is pictured in September 2008 in Poulton-le-Fylde working the 2C, a half-hourly extension from South Pier to Knott End that crosses the River Wyre via Shard Bridge.

A September 2008 view of the purple livery of Line 7 on Optare Excel 210 (T210 HCW), leaving Cleveleys for the Saltcotes Road terminus in Lytham.

The busy Line 11 with turquoise branding, incorporating what once was a service operated jointly by the Blackpool and Lytham St Annes municipal undertakings, was usually double-deck operated. This September 2008 view shows 324 (PN04 XDH), a TransBus Trident with East Lancs Myllennium Lolyne bodywork, arriving in Lytham from Cleveleys.

Just like Line 1, schools service double-deckers (in this case with lilac branding) were used on the seasonal Line 20 linking Marton Mere Holiday Park with Blackpool town centre, where ECW-bodied Leyland Olympian 402 (XAU 702Y), new to Trent, was standing in October 2005. Line 20 later became an open-top service with Olympians in City Sightseeing red.

Among the trams painted into a version of Metro Coastlines livery was English Electric 'Balloon' double-decker 713, new in 1934 and returned to service in 2005 after a three-year overhaul. This September 2008 view shows it approaching Gynn Square while heading south from Cleveleys to the Pleasure Beach. It has since gained an overall advertising livery and is retained as a heritage car.

The Lifestyle Line was a new service launched in July 2002 with funding from the government's Urban Bus Challenge, using six Blackpool Council-owned Optare Solos in a bespoke livery. In 2007 the service, no longer supported and greatly extended in length, morphed into Line 16 and received new Solos in a light blue livery, including 292 (YJ07 EJL) photographed leaving Fleetwood Ferry at the start of its convoluted route to Blackpool town centre.

ABOVE: *A few double-deckers were painted in a black and yellow pool livery, including 375 (M375 SCK), a Volvo Olympian with Northern Counties Palatine II body. In this September 2008 view, it was arriving in Cleveleys from St Annes on on Line 11.*

RIGHT: *The grey, yellow and mustard pool livery in April 2004 on Optare Delta-bodied DAF SB220 124 (J124 GRN).*

Newcastle was 'Atlantean City'. The corporation built up a large fleet of these rear-engined Leylands to replace trolleybuses, but 188 (188 JVK) with Metro-Cammell body was one of the first two delivered in 1960. It is outside the cathedral in St Nicholas Square in March 1968 on a cross-Tyne service to Gateshead. The corporation double-deckers behind it are Leyland Titans, a PD3/1 new in 1957 with Weymann Orion body and a 1948 Leyland-bodied PD2/1. The red and cream double-decker is an Alexander-bodied Daimler Fleetline in the Northern General-owned Tynemouth & District fleet. THE BUS ARCHIVE/ROY MARSHALL

Wish I was there

ROGER DAVIES first learnt about the bus scene beyond his native Cardiff from a wonderful series of illustrated reference books, but regrets that he didn't witness many of the fleets they described until their most distinctive vehicles and liveries had disappeared

The *British Bus Fleets* books of the 1950s and 1960s must have spurred on many enthusiasts. They certainly did me.

When my local one came out in 1963, no.18, South Wales, it opened up whole new vistas, if the likes of Aberdare and Gelligaer can be described as such, and explained many familiar vehicles. I was soon sorely tempted by the then other 19 in the series. A bit of judicious begging and a recent Christmas brought forth sufficient funds to complete the set in early 1965 and I was soon immersed.

I still think they offer the best geographical descriptions of the areas of the UK, far better and more accurately than the meaningless north and south so beloved of politicians. Topped up by monthly updates from *Buses Illustrated*, I soon became well acquainted with most parts of England and Wales and their buses at that time, something I retain today.

Over the years I came to visit most of the places covered but in some I missed the fleets as they were during the *BBF* days and there was often little left to see of that which I had learned

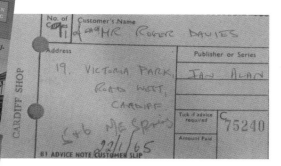

BELOW: *A fan of the six-wheel version, Roger Davies would love to have seen the 134 trolleybuses that Glasgow and Newcastle Corporations bought with Metro-Cammell bodies built to the design of London Transport's Q1 class. Glasgow TB1 (FYS 701), photographed at Riddrie in the north-east of the city in September 1962, was the first of 34 BUT 9641Ts new in 1949 when the system opened; there also were 30 Daimler CTM6s, while Newcastle had 70 BUTs. This version of Glasgow's green, cream and orange livery was unique to trolleybuses, with the green and cream areas above the lower cream band swapped round from the contemporary layout on motorbuses to disguise the accumulation of carbon deposits on trolleybus roofs.* IAIN MACGREGOR

about. A few fleets in particular I'm sorry I missed in their *BBF* years.

Trolleybus snobbery

I had ordered the items from a local bookstore and the order confirmation was (and still is) in the one on top of the plie, *BBF10 North-Eastern Area*, so it was tackled first. What leapt out of those pages was the fascinating scene to be found in Newcastle upon Tyne, somewhere a vast distance away for me. It was not until 1975 that I ventured to that fine city by which time it was well into PTE and National Bus Company days and getting Metro obsessed.

Today wandering its streets I wish I had experienced the superb and at that time dominant trolleybus system with its imposing vehicles. There

A November 1962 view of Liverpool Corporation A208 (VKB 806), one of 100 AEC Regent Vs with Metro-Cammell Orion bodies delivered between November 1956 and October 1959 to the operator's own specification, notably the window pans, four-bay construction and the pressed metal radiator grille. Glasgow specified a similar pressed metal grille on its 164 Regent Vs. It is in Carisbrooke Road, Walton next to a house with a baby carriage on the path and a red cradle in the doorway. The crew are likely in the garage canteen opposite. It is on a cross-city service to Penny Lane, more correctly Smithdown Place, but the former was always used on buses and trams well before the Beatles brought it to our attention in 1967.
THE BUS ARCHIVE/ROY MARSHALL

were many three-axle ones. Trolleybus snobs like me believe that is the correct number, but do acknowledge that some fine systems got by with one fewer. Indeed, Newcastle had a mix of both up to the end of buying new ones, which made it unusual and yet more interesting.

To add to it, Newcastle painted its buses yellow and cream with a maroon fleetname that looked as if it was hand painted. Given its heavy industrial heritage, what a wonderful, cheery choice to combat fog on the Tyne. How wonderful it would have been to have boarded a huge BUT with Metro-Cammell body echoing London's Q1 class and been whisked off silently to exotic Five Ball Lonnen. I've been there since, so know the truth.

But that was not all. The local BET company, Northern General, had all sorts of subsidiaries with their own identities, liveries and even vehicle choices. It appeared from afar as if whichever way you left Newcastle there was a different fleet. All of which gave the BET group a fascinating variety and endless interest for the enthusiast.

This was not true of the state owned Tilling group

and those do not appear on my wish list. Yet the huge one in the north-east, United, did have some pretty stunning operating areas. On top of all this, *BBF10* included an independent operator, Venture, running widely but centred around the Consett area and adjusting Newcastle Corporation's colours to its own requirements.

To add to the excitement, both Northern and Newcastle had been early converts to the Leyland Atlantean, indeed it was christened Atlantean City by enthusiasts. It is difficult to remember today what an incredible impact this bus design had, so it gave Newcastle a special bus buzz.

A whole different thing
Scotland was a whole different thing. At first it only had one *BBF*, no.20, Glasgow Corporation, and what a treasure trove that was. For a mere 3/- (15p), there was little you could not learn about this fascinating and, to south of the border eyes, unusual operator.

The rest of Scotland was covered in 1966 by two mighty tomes but their contents had not varied that much by the time I had ventured across Hadrian's

Wall in 1975. It was some years before I slipped through far outer suburbs of Glasgow and by then it was in the grip of a PTE.

None of these bodies scored in the livery stakes. Somehow even Tyne & Wear debased Newcastle Corporation's hue, but the original Greater Glasgow yellow, white and insipid green was awful, following the bold Corporation colours. And how I would have loved to see the streets of this elegant city heaving with strange and weird types glowing with their strong colours again often to the backdrop of a massive industrial heritage. It was nothing short of genius.

And here we had another splendid trolleybus system, albeit late in starting and criminally short in existence. Okay, so there were lots of two-axle jobs but the fleet was blessed with both experimental standee-type and very long single-deckers. How could I have resisted a trip to Mount Florida on 35ft of Burlingham-bodied single-deck trolley? I was lucky, a preserved one toured Cardiff, but it wasn't the same.

I was very late in discovering Glasgow and would have loved to have seen it with its own distinctive buses. Still, I did know copycat Halifax buses and how wonderful were they?

Centre of the world

In the 1960s there was nowhere like Liverpool. It was the centre of the world, the launchpad for the Beatles whose true impact is still not fully realised today. We all affected Liverpool accents, used the words and saw scenes of the city on our televisions.

Inevitably, Liverpool Corporation buses, the "Corpy", appeared memorably in the video for Penny Lane, which we all soon knew was a bus terminus. It was on the front of Corpy buses in those distinctive destination boxes. Mind you, there is a clip of John Lennon with a Routemaster. It may have been RM1414 on its visit but I somehow doubt it. The buses also appeared in the popular series *The Liver Birds* so it was as if we knew them well.

The Corpy favoured a rather fab green and latterly cream just around the window surrounds which I found groovy, attractive and, as I found out later in my career, very practical. They did terrible things with tin fronts, assembled bodies themselves, managing to make even the most elegant gawky. And they were a bit, well, basic. But I've only known Liverpool as it is today in its rejuvenated form and largely escaped the horrors of the PTE with its awful livery and obsession with turfing people off buses and on to trains.

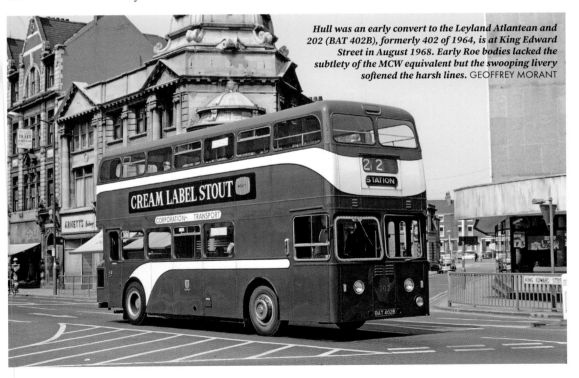

Hull was an early convert to the Leyland Atlantean and 202 (BAT 402B), formerly 402 of 1964, is at King Edward Street in August 1968. Early Roe bodies lacked the subtlety of the MCW equivalent but the swooping livery softened the harsh lines. GEOFFREY MORANT

East Yorkshire used a lighter blue for coaches including double-deckers built for limited stop services like the Hornsea Express on which 571 (MKH 80), a 1951 Leyland Titan PD2/12 with full-front Roe 50-seat body with Beverley Bar roof, was waiting in the bus station outside Hull Paragon railway station. The single-deck bus livery is behind. The British Rail advertisement next to the double-decker publicises the electrification of the London-Southampton-Bournemouth line from July 1967.
THE BUS ARCHIVE/ROY MARSHALL

I did visit the replica Cavern Club and listened to a guy singing Beatle songs and it was a delight But how I would have liked to see big ships on the Mersey, known the city as the Fab Four did and been surrounded by those dodgy buses.

Amazing blues

Blue buses were unusual. In south Wales we had Pontypridd, PUDC to all, and I was used to the fabulous bright blue Bradford buses that so cheered the city in its smoke stack stained period. But in Hull, all the buses were blue. How amazing is that? In addition it wasn't really called that; it is Kingston upon Hull and calling it Hull is a bit like calling Newcastle "Tyne".

And it's not even the major river. That's the Humber which is a bit like Sheffield named after the Sheaf rather than the Don. But Donfield would be too like Dronfield down the road. Back in Hull, the corporation bus fleet latterly entered into it by simply bunging "Corporation Transport" on the side just to join in the fun. And they were blue with swooping lines, not really a swooping lines man

myself, but it was a distinctive look.

Sadly, their trolleybuses had gone before I became better acquainted with the fleet but they did have one connection for me. A treasured possession was the splendid tome *Trolleybus Trails* by J Joyce which had a Hull Coronation-class trolleybus on the cover. At one term end when own books were allowed, I took it into school. We were supervised by a languages master called Aafon Morgan or, more commonly, Boris. He was a substantial. charming, brilliant man who could speak ten languages fluently.

At the end of the period he called me over and asked to see my book. I put it before him. He placed a huge, hirsute hand either side of it and gazed down. As mentioned, the bus merely stated "Corporation Transport", but Boris let out a sigh and said, "Hull". Never mind ten languages, I was in awe.

But there was more, the local BET operator, East Yorkshire, painted its buses blue too and its double-deckers had a strangely angled roof to fit under an arch called the Beverley Bar and thus was

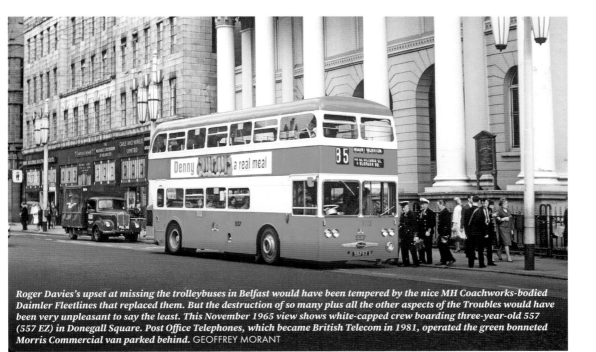

Roger Davies's upset at missing the trolleybuses in Belfast would have been tempered by the nice MH Coachworks-bodied Daimler Fleetlines that replaced them. But the destruction of so many plus all the other aspects of the Troubles would have been very unpleasant to say the least. This November 1965 view shows white-capped crew boarding three-year-old 557 (557 EZ) in Donegall Square. Post Office Telephones, which became British Telecom in 1981, operated the green bonneted Morris Commercial van parked behind. GEOFFREY MORANT

the style known throughout the land.

What with swoops , strange roofs and even paddle steamer ferries across the Humber, it must have been great to be surrounded by blue buses. By the time I made it to the Land of Green Ginger, the swoops had gone and NBC had crushed the blue and East Yorkshire buses were poppy red like all NBC buses in the county.

I'd have liked to be blue in Hull.

The province beyond BBFs

Somewhere untouched by *BBF*s was Northern Ireland. Tempting morsels appeared in *Buses Illustrated* particularly concerning Belfast Corporation. This enjoyed an individualistic look with local Harkness and MH Coachworks bodywork and also boasted a rather fabulous trolleybus system firmly based on three axles.

Rather like Scotland when viewed from the south, it had a whiff of difference about it with the added fission being that the "overseas" Ulster Transport Authority also had distinctive buses, many built in its own workshops and its dark green buses mixing with Belfast's red must have made an interesting scene. Then in 1967 the UTA was swept away by a blue tide of Ulsterbus which must also have been a fascinating period.

But the trolleybuses were the main attraction

and what a system it was. Destinations again had a delightfully unusual ring about them and I would not have resisted leaping on one headed off to the impressive parliament building at Stormont. The system was on the way out, but my sadness was eased by the replacements being, in my view, very smart MH Coachworks-bodied Daimler Fleetlines and I felt I could get along with that.

And it almost came to pass. I received an excellent offer from Queens University Belfast which I should easily have attained. I didn't and was briefly saddened. I'd have gone up in October 1968 so would have missed the trolleybuses by five months. But we have something in common. We both missed the Troubles by the skin of our teeth.

I have visited all these places now, many times, and know them pretty well; and all are convenient for me these days. Belfast is a firm favourite. For those of my age, the thought of sitting by a window in the Europa hotel seemed inconceivable. Glasgow is a revelation, totally different from Edinburgh. Newcastle has an air of self-containment providing for all needs, while Liverpool shows how a city can be saved from the brink. Hull is no longer blue.

Many things about them have improved, but the buses could be anywhere and add no unique identity to their streets. I cannot help missing their presence. ∎

ABOVE: *Like many big city fleets, Birmingham's weas predominantly double-deck, but it had a limited requirement for single-deckers met from 1950 mainly by 30 of these Leyland Tiger PS2s with 34-seat Weymann bodies. This June 1965 view of 2258 (JOJ 258) in Bournville Lane shows one reason why nothing taller could operate on route 27. Besides the 10ft clearance beneath that railway bridge, another at Northfield also precluded the use of double-deckers. New Marshall-bodied Daimler Fleetlines took their place that year but this was one of a dozen PS2s converted for one-man operation and kept for four more years. Among the colourful advertisements is one for Cadbury's chocolate, manufactured in Bournville.* IAIN MACGREGOR

The many colours of the
West Midlands

Birmingham and the Black Country invested civic pride in their municipal bus fleets with identities their modern day successor has happily acknowledged

Most of the double-deckers that Wolverhampton bought between 1948 and 1967 were built in the town by Guy Motors, Its 1954 intake included seven Arab IVs with preselector gearboxes and 56-seat Metro-Cammell Orion bodies, among them 580 (KJW 580) photographed in 1962 at Victoria Square, near the railway station. Like most rear-entrance double-deckers in the Birmingham fleet, these also had a straight staircase.
IAIN MACGREGOR

The four municipal fleets at the heart of the West Midlands — Birmingham, Walsall, West Bromwich and Wolverhampton — had their own distinct identities when Iain MacGregor visited them in the 1960s, which were lost when they were amalgamated into the newly created West Midlands PTE in October 1969.

Three of them had blue liveries. Birmingham City Transport, with around 1,700 vehicles the largest of all British municipal bus operators, painted them dark blue and cream, Walsall's were blue from top to bottom, relieved by thin horizontal gold bands and West Brom appeared to pay homage to both of its neighbours, with two shades of blue relieved cream, lined out delicately in black and gold. Its newest double-deckers were cream with token bands of light blue, but they were in the minority.

Wolverhampton stood apart, with combinations of apple green and primrose, some vehicles having

Walsall general manager Edgley Cox was an innovative engineer unafraid to operate a highly mixed fleet and eager to try out new designs. He carried out an extended evaluation of one of Leyland's prototype rear-engined double-deckers in the 1950s and bought his first production example, Leyland Atlantean 841 (841 FDH), in September 1959. It had a 74-seat lowheight Weymann body with nearside sunken gangway towards the rear of the top deck, an arrangement that allowed double-deckers to ply routes with low bridges. Visible above the shelter to the right, in the town's bus station in September 1962, are the booms of one of Walsall's trolleybuses, the last of which survived long enough to be the only ones operated by a PTE. IAIN MACGREGOR

ABOVE: *West Bromwich was one of the first operators outside Scotland to buy Alexander bodywork, fitted in 1953 in place of the wartime utility bodies on seven Daimler CWA6s and a recycled prewar body on a 1947 CWD6. This September 1962 view in the High Street — then a busy centre with independent retailers, regional and national chains — shows CWA6 126 (BEA 736), new in 1945 with a Duple body. Its original 7.7litre AEC engine was replaced by a five-cylinder Gardner 5LW. The staff of Preedy's, a Midlands tobacconist with over 40 branches, have just pulled open the shop's canvas awning.* IAIN MACGREGOR

BELOW: *National Express West Midlands has painted 4722 (BU07 LGY), an Alexander Dennis Enviro400, in traditional Birmingham City Transport livery of dark blue and cream with a khaki roof, but without a coat of arms. The khaki roof was introduced in wartime to make bus roofs less visible to enemy aircraft when parked outside and remained part of the livery until the PTE took over.* RICHARD GODFREY

greater proportions of primrose than others.

The PTE and its successors — including today's National Express West Midlands — are proud of their heritage and several times in subsequent decades have painted modern vehicles in the colours once strongly identified with the communities they served. ∎

After operation by Stagecoach for several years, the 400-series West Hunts services returned to Whippet in April 2011. They were usually operated by coaches, before the use of low-floor buses became mandatory, because many of the remote rural roads in Huntingdonshire had uneven surfaces considered unsuitable for such vehicles. WC203 (H19 WCL), a Jonckheere Mistral-bodied Volvo B10M-62, negotiates the single-track road between Upton and Buckworth on April 20, 2015 while operating the circuitous Mondays-only 402 service from St Ives to Huntingdon. This coach was new in 2001 to Shearings, as its 320 (Y391 KBN).

Whippet shows its pedigree

JOHN ROBINSON pays a photographic tribute to one of the longest surviving independent operators in the east of England — one that has changed hands twice in recent years

Whippet Coaches is one of the few surviving independent operators of local bus services from the years before deregulation in 1986.

It was established in 1919 when bicycle salesman Henry Lee began operations from the village of Graveley in Huntingdonshire with a Model T Ford van the local blacksmith had converted into a bus.

Its first service was from Graveley to the market town of St Neots. It followed this later with a service linking Hilton and St Ives with Cambridge. Growth was gradual with only a few vehicles acquired before World War Two. The opening of many Royal Air Force bases in the area during the war created a requirement to transport forces personnel in the area and the growth of Whippet accelerated, leading to it relocate to nearby Hilton.

The fleet was entirely single-deck until January 1955 when the first double-decker, a 1943 ex-Huddersfield Corporation Daimler CWA6, entered service. Since then, until recently, double-deckers were a feature of the fleet. Several were purchased new, the first being a smart Willowbrook-bodied Leyland Atlantean which arrived in 1966.

Whippet was the first operator in the Eastern

Traffic Area to purchase Volvos when six B58s with Plaxton Panorama Elite Express bodywork, which with bus entrance doors, entered service in 1973 for use on local bus work as well as coaching. It has run Volvos ever since then Volvos.

Whippet continued to expand its local bus operations together with its school contracts and in 1977 moved into a new, larger depot at Fenstanton, on the outskirts of St Ives. In 2009 it moved again to a modern depot at Swavesey, the Fenstanton premises being acquired by Stagecoach as a replacement for its Huntingdon depot. The Fenstanton site meant that Stagecoach was now strategically placed for its operations on the then soon-to-be-opened Cambridgeshire guided busway, Whippet being the only other operator on the busway.

In November 2014, after 95 years' continuous ownership, the Lee family sold Whippet to Tower Transit, the London arm of an Australian company which had come to Britain when it purchased part of First's London operations in June the previous year.

The change of ownership introduced London-style fleetnumbers with separate series for coaches (WC), double-deckers (WD), single-deckers (WS)

and guided buses (WG).Operation by Tower Transit was short-lived, however, as in November 2018 ownership changed to Ascendal, a formed out of a de-merger from Tower Transit.

Emphasis on express coaching

Since 2014, the main emphasis has been on express coaching, with around half the fleet being coaches. The local bus service network has reduced significantly to the extent that Whippet no longer serves St Ives, a main hub of its operations for the best part of 100 years, following its withdrawal of Busway service C between St Ives and Cambridge in November 2018.

The Covid-19 global pandemic also has had a fundamental effect since March 2020. National Express, for whom Whippet was a contractor, ceased operating coaches for several months at the same time as patronage on local bus services was reduced drastically.

The last double-deckers, Wright Eclipse Gemini-bodied Volvo B7TLs cascaded from Tower Transit, were withdrawn in late 2020, making the fleet all single-deck again for the first time in 65 years.

National Express had acquired some substantial coach operating companies in southern and central England and began to operate more services directly. Whippet ceased to be a contractor in 2021 and that April started working with German-owned Flixbus, which was establishing routes in competition with National Express and Stagecoach's Megabus business.

Whippet coaches could now be seen operating services from cities including Bradford, Bristol and Swansea to London Victoria using the Caetano Levante-bodied Scanias previously used on the National Express work.

While it operated approximately 36 local bus services in 2000, these were down to eight by 2020. However, Whippet took over some services previously operated by Centrebus in the Corby and Kettering areas in October 2019 following the closure of its Corby depot. At the same time, it introduced a service linking Huntingdon and Corby which it absorbed into existing service X3 (Cambridge-Huntingdon) in August 2020 with some journeys extended to Corby.

I began to photograph Whippet after a job move to Huntingdonshire at the end of 1996. Although I returned to north-west England in 2020, I have made several return visits to cover some of its latest acquisitions for this feature.

During those 25 years, the livery has changed many times, and even what was "standard" at any time often exhibited detail differences in its application between vehicles. Also, many used vehicles entered service before they were repainting in Whippet livery — or were never re-painted at all — which added to the photographic appeal of this operator. ∎

Whippet's loyalty to Volvo prompted its purchase of new and secondhand B10M-based Citybus double-deckers with mid underfloor engine. F117 PHM was one of two with dual-door Alexander AV-type bodies acquired from Arriva London in early 2003 and new to Grey-Green in 1998. This view from December 17, 2003 shows it in the Oxmoor Estate in Huntington, while operating service 1A to Cambridge.

Wearing the livery introduced in 2004, G823 UMU, the first of a pair of Northern Counties-bodied Volvo Citybuses purchased new in 1989, heads out of Drummer Street bus station, Cambridge in torrential rain while operating service 196 to Waterbeach on January 13, 2010; another new vehicle of the same type arrived the following year registered H303 CAV. Stagecoach Volvo Olympian 16025 (P825 GMU), with Northern Counties Palatine body, follows close behind. It was new to Stagecoach East London in 1996 as its VN25.

Among several Alexander RL-bodied Leyland Olympians acquired from various Stagecoach fleets was K713 ASC, new to Fife Scottish in 1992 and transferred to United Counties in 1994. This was allocated fleetnumber WD423 following the sale to Tower Transit. Here it stands in Huntingdon bus station on July 15, 2014 alongside Whippet's smart Volvo FL10 recovery truck J100 SEA. Previously in a short-lived cream livery with dark blue skirt and large fleetnames, it was repainted in the unique scheme shown here, combining aspects of the existing 90th anniversary livery and the new allover blue. Because Whippet didn't want an older bus to be the first in the new livery, the hybrid layout shown here was devised as a one-off.

Between 1982 and 1989, Whippet amassed around 25 Scania BR111DH-based MCW Metropolitans from several sources. The last one in service (aside from one converted to open-top) was KJD 271P, new as London Transport MD71 and photographed in Buttsgrove Way, Oxmoor in August 1998 on service 1A. Remarkably, upon withdrawal it passed to Imperial Coaches, Rainham, Essex for further service where I had the pleasure of driving it once; the power was awesome. No wonder the fuel consumption of Metropolitans was so high.

Following on from the Metropolitans, the secondhand double-decker of choice was the Leyland Titan with 18 joining the fleet between 1993 and 1997, all originating with London Transport. This is former London Buses T283 (KYN 283X), operating the Oxmoor Estate Metro 16 service around 1998. It was in the livery used before the introduction in 1996 of the more complex design carried by the Metropolitan.

Passing through the picturesque village of Houghton on April 23, 2009 on service 1A from Huntingdon to Cambridge was L56 UNS, one of a pair of Northern Counties Paladin-bodied Volvo B10Bs dating from 1993 and acquired from Whitelaw, Stonehouse, South Lanarkshire in September 2001.

V293 UVY, later allocated fleetnumber WS309, was an Alexander ALX300-bodied Volvo B10BLE new to Reliance, Sutton-on-the-Forest, North Yorkshire in 2000. Rapeseed was flowering on April 30, 2011 as it left Stonely with the afternoon Saturday-only 401 service from Grafham to Huntingdon.

Four new East Lancs-bodied Volvos entered service in September 2001. One was a B7TL double-decker, while the other three were B6BLEs with Spryte bodywork. This view on May 1, 2015 shows WS306 (FE51 RCU) in Cambridge Road, Godmanchester, operating service 5 from Huntingdon to St Ives. With the opening of the new alignment of the A14 between Huntingdon and Cambridge in December 2019, the original part of the A14 on the bridge behind the bus was downgraded into a local distributor road reclassified as the A1307.

Another ex-Stagecoach vehicle owned was K702 DAO, from the first batch of 90 a Volvo B10M-55s with Alexander PS-type bodywork new to the Cumberland fleet in 1992. The effects of the wintry weather were all too apparent on the side panels on December 11, 2010 as darkness fell in Market Square, St Neots where it was preparing to depart on service 28 to Gamlingay.

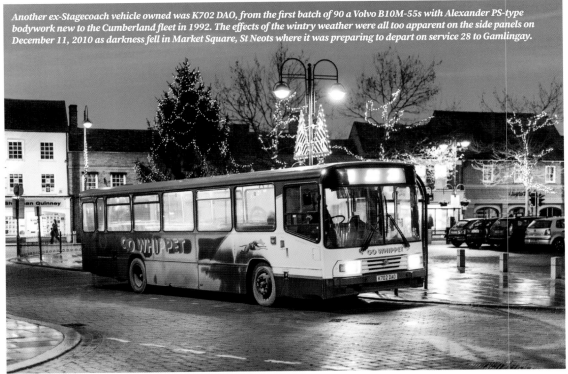

The Whippet Puppy brand was introduced in 2015 on four smaller single-deckers transferred into the fleet from Impact of Perivale, another business then owned by Tower Transit. Three were Alexander Dennis Enviro200s, while the fourth was this Chinese-built King Long XMQ6900 which remained white for its stay and was numbered WS323 (BX14 KSF). It was in Kimbolton High Street on August 5, 2016 when it was operating the 17:40 service 400 journey from Huntingdon to Spaldwick.

Four Volvo B7RLEs with Wright Eclipse Urban bodywork were acquired from Lothian Country in 2020, with some operated initially in their former owner's green and cream. WS341 (SN04 NHJ), formerly Lothian 118, had been repainted in the new livery (but with more yellow at the front than others of the type) when photographed at Stonely on April 15, 2021 operating the 07:45 service 400 from Spaldwick to Huntingdon. This was originally a guided bus with Lothian, used on the short section of busway built on the west of the city and active between December 2004 and January 2009 before it was incorporated within the new Edinburgh Trams route linking the city centre and airport.

Whippet ceased operating on the main Cambridgeshire guided busway between St Ives and Cambridge in November 2018 but continued to operate on the shorter section between Cambridge railway station and Addenbrooke's Hospital with the Universal-branded service U linking Eddington, in the west of the city near the Madingley Road park-&-ride, on normal roads and using the busway to reach the hospital's the Biomedical Campus. This is WG106 (BT66 MVF), one of seven Volvo B8RLEs with Wright Eclipse 3 bodywork purchased new for this service in 2016, passing under Long Road as it heads away from the city. This section of the busway is built partially on the trackbed of the former Cambridge-Oxford line which is set to be re-opened, but on a new route between Cambridge and Bedford.

Whippet bought three Plaxton Centro-bodied Volvo B7RLEs to operate on the Busway when it opened in 2011. It replaced them with newer Wright-bodied Volvos but the combination reappeared in the fleet late in 2019 with the acquisition of another pair. They were repainted the following August into the new livery incorporating Whippet Express branding for service X3 which had been enhanced with further journeys extended to Corby, replacing the previous service 18 between Huntingdon and Corby introduced the previous October. By a quirk of scheduling, WS328 (YX59 BZK) was operating the West Hunts services on October 9, 2020 while sister vehicle WS327 was operating the X3 along with an unbranded single-decker. WS328 waits by a repurposed traditional telephone kiosk in The Avenue in Leighton Bromswold after arriving on the 12:30 service 401 from Huntingdon, and just before returning to Huntingdon on the direct route along the A14. Both were among six new to Veolia Transport in 2009 for a Leicester park-&-ride contract.

Before 1995, Kyle of Lochalsh was the westernmost point you could reach on the A87 without taking a ferry to Kyleakin on the Isle of Skye. This August 1987 picture shows an eastbound Plaxton Paramount-bodied Volvo B10M of Park's of Hamilton pulling away from the Caledonian MacBrayne ferry Lochalsh, one of two on the crossing – complete with errant seagull somewhere between camera and windscreen. The coach was operating on behalf of Trafalgar Tours – which, like Park's, was still active in 2021. A pair of larger ferries replaced these in 1991, but the Skye bridge opened four years later, and scenes like this became part of history.

Ends of the Earth

PETER ROWLANDS takes it to the limit in this whistle-stop tour round some of the more remote parts of the United Kingdom that he has visited in more than 40 years of bus and coach photography

You have to go out of your way to visit some places in Britain. They are simply not on the way to anywhere else.

The most obvious examples are Land's End and John O'Groats, but there are plenty of others, too: St Davids, for instance, at the end of the road heading west across south Wales; and Barrow-in-Furness, perched on the end of the Furness peninsula in south-west Cumbria.

Opposite Barrow across Morecambe Bay is Fleetwood, another end-of-the-line town. It lies at the northern tip of the Fylde peninsula, with the bay to the north, the Irish Sea to the west and the river Wyre to the east. The only land route in and out is south.

This article celebrates such places and the buses that have served them. In many places I have found double-deckers and full-sized single-deckers as well as short buses, narrow buses and minibuses, all chosen to suit the loadings and the roads they would encounter on their travels.

Not all the places I have chosen are literally at the end of the road, but most of them have the distinction of being the most extreme points in their area. Llandudno, for instance, has several routes running in and out of it, but there is nothing else beyond it except the Great Orme peninsula. Beachy Head is by no means the southernmost point in Britain, but it certainly carries that honour for East Sussex.

What all these places have in common is a sense of being at the edge of something. Happily in most cases they seem to thrive on it, often attracting visitors – and bus passengers – through their very remoteness. ∎

Oban, at the western end of the A85, has the deceptive air of being a substantial town – perhaps reflecting the fact that in normal times its modest population of around 9,000 can be almost tripled by the tourist trade, and there is a constant flow of ferry traffic to and from the Western Isles. The restaurant above the Edinburgh Woollen Mill advertises the attraction of a "Scottish Show". Photographed in August 1986 passing Oban Bay on George Street (part of the A85), this compact front-engined Bedford SB5 has a 39-seat Duple Dominant body suited to the tight clearances on some of the roads in the area. LF Stewart was based in Dalavich, a village only 12miles from Oban as the crow flies, but 26miles and well over an hour away via a circuitous route round the mountainous interior.

In glorious summer sunshine, this Daimler Fleetline of Highland Omnibuses waits at John O'Groats to start the 28mile return journey along Scotland's northern coast to Thurso. It was new to Alexander (Fife) in 1971, and although smart, its boxy ECW body looked dated by August 1986. Its claim to be the "Best Bus Around" perhaps smacks of wishful thinking. Nonetheless, it went on to have a further life with Hollis of Queensferry in north Wales.

Seahouses lies on a natural harbour on the Northumberland coast, 50miles north of Newcastle upon Tyne. This Plaxton Paramount-bodied Volvo B10M was on the short stretch of sea front in the town. It was new to Wallace Arnold in 1990, but by August 1996 was in the colours of short-lived East Yorkshire Travel, renamed National Holidays the following year and sold, ironically, to Wallace Arnold in 2001. The Viking venue celebrated in the sign behind the coach is long gone, though a chic residential block called The Viking now stands not far from this location.

The Giant's Causeway – an array of interlocking hexagonal basalt columns – lies just short of the northernmost point on mainland Northern Ireland, so is in the United Kingdom rather than Great Britain. In November 1997, Flexibus (part of Ulsterbus and then Translink) was running this 26-seat Wright TS-bodied Mercedes-Benz 811D midibus on a short shuttle service for tourists. There were dozens of Mercedes-Benz midibuses in the combined Ulsterbus-Flexibus fleet, but this particular configuration was unique, built for this service, with a wheelchair bay at the rear, reached by a ramp in the nearside door. The National Trust visitor centre seen here burned down in 2000 and was eventually replaced 12 years later.

South Shields occupies a corner of the north-east England coastline on the south bank of the Tyne and is the end of the line for a branch of the Tyne & Wear Metro. The bridge is probably the only part of this scene that has survived a recent massive redevelopment and creation of a major transport interchange. Busways had become part of Stagecoach when this three-year-old Plaxton Pointer-bodied Dennis Dart was photographed in August 1996. It would eventually gain Stagecoach's striped livery, and in later life acquired at least half a dozen other liveries with operators in Perth, Huddersfield and Stoke-on-Trent.

Whitehaven is the westernmost town in Cumbria and in the 18th century was a major Atlantic seaport. In June 1983 it was still served by Cumberland Motor Services, whose ECW-bodied Bristol VRT was in a parking area across the road from the town's bus station alongside Leyland Nationals and an incomplete Bristol RELL. The view from the houses above in St George's Terrace is now marred by a Tesco car park and the buses have gone, while the Art Deco bus station, which stood derelict for more than ten years, is being converted into office space and a restaurant. The VRT was later exported to Germany.

BELOW: *Fifty meandering miles west of the M6, the shipbuilding centre of Barrow-in-Furness must qualify as one of the remotest substantial towns in Britain. It has a population of over 50,000 and until 1989, when Stagecoach stepped in, had its own municipal bus operation. Barrow was mostly loyal to northern bodybuilders, but this Leyland Leopard from 1966 was one of five with bodywork by Hampshire-based Strachans featuring a classic BET-style front end. This was June 1983.*

ABOVE: *Fleetwood lies at the north end of the Fylde peninsula, and the Esplanade, behind this Metro-Cammell Weymann-bodied Leyland Titan PD3A/1, is the northernmost point on it. Blackpool Corporation had 90 buses built broadly to this design. This late example, dating from 1967, was photographed in September 1983. It remained in service for another five years, and survives in preservation as a working hire bus. A prewar Railcoach tram is in the background; the Blackpool tram route also survives, still threading its way through some of the town's main streets but with modern articulated vehicles.*

East Yorkshire bought more than 30 of these Park Royal-bodied AEC Renowns, adopted in 1964 after the similar-looking but integral Bridgemaster was discontinued. This one is in Bridlington, the most easterly of the main resort towns on the Yorkshire coast. The vestigial Beverley Bar pinched-in roof profile, shown clearly here, was a long-standing East Yorkshire feature, designed to allow clearance under the low arch of the North Bar in Beverley, between Bridlington and Hull. Originally blue, this 1965 bus was in National Bus Company poppy red in 1977. It only lasted another couple of years.

The linked towns of Grimsby and Cleethorpes lie at the eastern end of the A180, 40miles east of the M18. This Alexander RH-bodied Dennis Dominator, photographed in May 1990, is one of seven acquired by the arm's-length Grimsby-Cleethorpes Transport, which had adopted an orange and white livery three years earlier. The two towns' crests are displayed beside the destination indicator (Grimsby's is to the left in this picture). Stagecoach purchased the operation in 1993, and the bus gained its blue, red and orange stripes.

Llandudno, perhaps the best-known tourist town on the north Wales coast, has retained much of its Victorian charm. Unlike Rhyl, Prestatyn and Colwyn Bay, which lie on a continuous coastal ribbon, it sits out on a limb that ends with the Great Orme, a limestone headland served by Britain's only surviving cable tramway. Arriva was a keen buyer of VDL's SB200 chassis, and this Wright Pulsar-bodied example was negotiating Mostyn Street in May 2011, followed by a Volvo B7RLE with similar Eclipse Urban bodywork.

An Eastern Counties Bristol VRT with locally-built ECW bodywork crosses the bascule bridge over Lake Lothing, part of Lowestoft harbour, in March 1990, when it was 11 years old. An elaborate system of lane controls and lifting barriers manages access and traffic flow across the bridge, which connects the two halves of the town. Eastern Counties had been privatised three years before, and adopted this deep red colour scheme with cream and orange bands. The company was acquired by GRT (later FirstBus) in 1994. Lowestoft is the most easterly town in the British Isles.

BELOW: *Not quite as far east as Lowestoft and 9miles farther north, Great Yarmouth bought from a variety of bodybuilders over the years, but only introduced locally-built ECW bodywork on its 1973 batch of AEC Swifts. Before that, it acquired 21 Willowbrook-bodied Swifts, including this example from 1970, which was catching January sunshine in 1985 when Eastern Counties still painted its buses in NBC poppy red. First acquired the town's municipal bus company in 1996.*

ABOVE: *The A487 between Haverfordwest and St Davids in south-west Wales runs briefly alongside St Brides Bay, where it acquires the name Wood Hill. This DAF SB220-based Optare Delta, originally with British Airports Authority at Gatwick, was operated by Richards Bros., then as now a leading bus operator in the area, and was heading north in July 2001. St Davids, technically a city, is Britain's smallest, with a population of under 2,000, and also its most westerly – though some people make that claim for Truro in Cornwall.*

The pub signs leave little doubt as to the location of this picture, which was taken in August 2019. The Alexander ALX400-bodied Volvo B7TL was new to Arriva London South, and it was cutting through a sea fret while in service with Seaford & District, an operator based in Ringmer, near Lewes. At 530ft, Beachy Head is the highest chalk cliff in England, though tourists can only see the top of it from the bus. Beachy Head is the southernmost point in East Sussex. Following the sale of the main part of its business to The Big Lemon at the beginning of 2021, the Eastbourne Sightseeing service continues in the name of a new company, Seven Sisters Bus & Coach.

Looking elegant but dated by August 1981, this front-engined Bedford SB5 coach was at Shanklin station, the southernmost stop on the Isle of Wight railway, which until 2020 was operated with ex-London Transport deep-level tube trains. The coach was new to local operator Moss of Sandown in 1963, and is one of a small number with a front chassis extension by Yeates of Loughborough, allowing the passenger door to be placed ahead of the front axle. Yeates also built the stylish 44-seat Fiesta FE44 body, which was among the last from the company before its bodybuilding business closed in 1963.

Climbing westwards out of Lyme Regis, this East Lancs-bodied Scania N94 OmniDekka of First Hampshire & Dorset was just a year old when photographed in July 2005. It carries the name Mary Anning, a world famous 19th-century palaeontologist associated with research into the Jurassic Coast fossil beds. The Coastlinx X53 was an impressive 90mile route between Poole and Exeter via Weymouth, which is the most southerly town on this stretch of coast. Today's remnant of the service covers just the central section between Weymouth and Axminster, north of Lyme.

The adjacent towns of Lynton and Lynmouth are the most northerly in Devon, though Foreland Point, 3miles to the east, juts some way farther out into the Bristol Channel. This TransBus Mini Pointer Dart of Filers Travel is in Lynton at the top of the water-powered cliff railway that connects the two towns. It was new to Arriva Midlands North in 2003, and was photographed in July 2011. Ilfracombe-based Filers is still an active transport operator in north-west Devon.

The heat haze is almost palpable in this summer 1991 shot of a five-year-old Mercedes-Benz L608D midibus. It is picking up what looks like a full load for its 19 seats in Penzance, England's westernmost town, with the tidal island of St Michael's Mount in the background. Western National had more than 80 of these Reeve Burgess Mercedes conversions, and in total ran more than 200 Mercedes-Benz midibuses – a reflection of the massive lurch to small buses in the mid-1980s in anticipation of privatisation and deregulation.

A **daring** day out to **Derry**

The Lough Swilly station at Letterkenny with a variety of single-deck Leylands parked outside. On the left is Leopard L2 140 (NZE 585), new in 1964 to CIÉ from whom it was on extended loan. Tiger Cub 82 (ZP 4360), with roof rack and rear ladder visible, was one of four bought new in 1957. Situated beside the County Donegal Railway station, the site was sold off by the Swilly and now sits buried under a supermarket. PICTURES BY HUGH DOUGHERTY EXCEPT WHERE STATED OTHERWISE

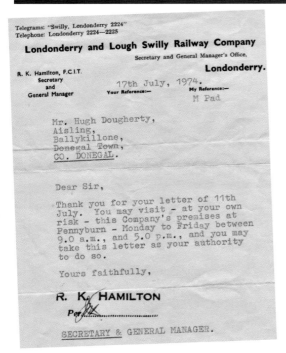

The letter granting Hugh Dougherty permission to visit the Pennyburn headquarters.

HUGH DOUGHERTY recalls a holiday of nearly 50 years ago when his enthusiasm for the Lough Swilly's buses twice in one day attracted the suspicions of army personnel at the height of Northern Ireland's Troubles

t's July 31, 1974, and I'm on holiday with my parents at Laghey, in the ancestral homeland of Donegal. My fiancée came over for the first two weeks, but she's back in Glasgow, and phoning her from pre-dial Donegal is a trial of patience and sanity. The woman on the switchboard in Laghey post office knows we're missing one another. And so does most of the townland…

Then there's the lure of the Lough Swilly buses, which I'd long wanted to know more about, having spotted them over many years in north Donegal. Now, visiting their headquarters at Pennyburn in Derry seems like a good move. It would offer a trip over the former County Donegal Railways, by 1974 CIÉ, routes from Laghey to Letterkenny and a Swilly bus from there into the Maiden City itself.

Leyland Tiger Cub 81 (ZP4359), bought new in 1957 with Weymann body assembled in Ireland by Ryan Coachbuilders, sitting between duties at Letterkenny station, with an E-class CIÉ Leopard, newly arrived from Strabane on what was a County Donegal Railways service until 1971, outside the station building.

And there was an ulterior motive, for, up in the North they had dial phones and coinboxes. I could phone my wife-to-be from Derry without difficulty, visit Pennyburn, which had been the company headquarters since the earliest days of the Swilly's origins as a railway company, have a chat with management, see the company in action and get back to Laghey, all on the same day.

So I wrote to the L&LSR, seeking permission to visit Pennyburn, and a reply came back on a genuine Londonderry & Lough Swilly Railway letterhead, signed by the general manager himself, granting permission to visit, at my own risk of course, despite all that was going on in Derry.

Going from Donegal to Derry in those days by bus was an adventure, not because CIÉ and Lough Swilly ran anything but an efficient service, but crossing the border from the Irish Republic into Northern Ireland was subject to British Army checks. Coming from the Republic for the day, being 23, having a name and face like mine, were all possible problems, but for a young buck like me,

Centre of this view at Pennyburn is 115 (FCK 887), one of five 1953 Saunders Roe-bodied Leyland Tiger Cubs bought ex-Ribble in 1969, which spent most of its time on schools work with the Swilly until withdrawal in 1979. When used, route number boxes often displayed the fleetnumber. On the right is one of a pair of 1970 Plaxton Panorama Elite-bodied Bristol LHL6Ls which were the last vehicles bought new. One of these operated the Letterkenny-Glasgow service when it began.

The classic Lough Swilly postwar bus was the centre-entrance Saunders Roe-bodied Leyland Royal Tiger of which eight were bought new between 1951 and 1953. Last to arrive was 78, registered in Donegal when new as FZP 391 and re-registered UI 5726 in Co. Londonderry. It still had five years of service ahead of it in 1974.

there was a frisson of danger.

Off I went on the 11.00 Sligo-Derry service to Ballybofey on a CIÉ C-class Leyland Leopard, a bus never suited to the then rough Donegal roads, thanks to its airbag suspension.

We arrived at 11.35 with the connection leaving, in the shape of a trusty E-class Leopard, for Letterkenny at 11.40, so I had no time to look round the old CDR depot at Stranorlar. But with the CIÉ bus due into Letterkenny at 12.25, and the Swilly connection to Derry due away at 13.25, I had time to see the former CDR and L&LSR stations, still giving in use as bus stations; the Swilly also ran a maintenance garage there for its buses and lorries.

Government rescue operation

At Letterkenny, there were ex-CIÉ Leopards, transferred to the Swilly as part of an Irish government rescue operation, given that the company was nearly bankrupt. Rumours were rife that the Swilly was about the shut up shop or be taken over by CIÉ, with the joint fleet being maintained at Stranorlar, once the HQ of the County Donegal Railways, the LSR's great rival.

The troubles just over the border in Derry hadn't helped either, but talking to staff at Letterkenny, I got the impression that morale wasn't too bad, and that the company's summer-only express service to Glasgow, operated jointly with Western SMT, was doing quite well in the circumstances.

Letterkenny was the hub of the Lough Swilly system in 1974, with services to Derry, Churchill, Burtonport, Fanad, Dungloe, Rosapenna and Downings, most routes still having three out and back journeys, some with a Sunday service too, and conductors, mail, newspapers and parcel traffic still much in evidence.

Behind the scenes, it was fighting for survival, battling an upsurge in car ownership, the near collapse of tourism because of the Troubles, and fierce competition from local operators, especially on the lucrative Donegal-Glasgow run.

Manager Ronnie Hamilton, who had signed my letter giving me permission to visit Pennyburn, was juggling keeping the service going with a fleet that included the classic Swilly bus, Saunders Roe-bodied Leyland Royal Tigers dating from 1953, while imploring both the Dublin and Stormont governments for aid.

Man with a suitcase

All that was at the back of my mind as I noticed some ex-CIÉ Leopards, freshly sprayed in the Swilly's then new brownish-red and cream zig-zag livery, and on hire from the Republic's national operator, as aid-in-kind from the Dublin government, to keep the wheels turning, especially as the L&LSR was responsible for school transport in its area, sub-contracted from CIÉ.

My look around finished when one of the Royal Tigers bounced into the station yard. It had covered the Burtonport line's route, leaving Dungloe at 10.00

and arriving in Letterkenny at 13.30, to almost the same timings as the train the bus replaced in 1940.

A few passengers, including one besuited man, by himself with an ancient suitcase, clambered aboard our Derry-bound double-decker, Leyland Titan PD3 no.68, a 1959-built, Roe-bodied 72-seater which was acquired by the Swilly from Kippax & District in 1968, and which was to pound the Derry-Letterkenny, Derry-Buncrana, and Derry-Moville routes, plus some school bus work, until 1982.

Our conductor, a student on for the summer, issued me with my 83p excursion return, using his vintage insert Setright machine, converted to decimal currency in 1971. Sterling mixed freely with Irish coins around the border area then, long before Punts and Euros; the expense of operating in a two-currency area would come later.

Towards the border checkpoint

We shot along the narrow main road to Derry, with superb views of Lough Swilly and the Dougherty Castle at Burt (not this branch of the family's noble seat) from my top-deck seat, and passed an outbound ex-CIÉ E-class Leopard heading from Dungloe, conductor ready to deal with parcels traffic, mails and newspapers, all of which made up a big part of the company's revenue.

All went well until Killea, just outside Derry, for there, guns bristling, a British Army checkpoint searched traffic coming from Donegal. So, it was all off the bus, with all the young men, me included, lined up alongside, pushed in the back, legs kicked apart, and made to balance against the lower deck panels on our finger tips.

The driver was told gruffly to get out his cab and the conductor had his waybill ripped up and tossed into the bushes. I was spun round, and a soldier, who was flicking through a series of photographs of suspects, asked me for some form of identity.

I produced my driving licence, with its Glasgow address, and that was enough to send him into a tirade. "A Fenian from Glasgow on a bus from Donegal," he screamed. "Wait there."

So I stood with the others as the Leyland diesel turned over slowly, and the driver lit up a philosophical fag as he could see we were in for a long wait. The suited man from Gweedore, who had joined us at Letterkenny off the Burtonport bus, and who was carrying the old fashioned suitcase, had also attracted the military's attention.

He pleaded that he was getting the train at Derry to make the boat connection for Stranraer and train for Glasgow, and that was enough for the sergeant to decide that the bus could sit at Killea long enough to ensure that this man missed his train at Derry.

Eventually we were allowed to go, but not before the troops had ascertained that I was not Hugh Doherty, the Balcombe Street bomber who,

Aid-in-kind from the Irish government included 138 (EZH 235), ex-CIÉ 36ft (11m) Leyland Leopard C235 with Metal Sections body built at the Spa Road works in Dublin. It which served with the Swilly from 1973 to 1981.

Also in the Swilly fleet at the time of Hugh Dougherty's visit was 88 (700 DTH), a Willowbrook-bodied AEC Renown new to West Wales of Tycroes in 1963. It had just been acquired when photographed in Derry in June 1968 and was kept until 1976.
IAIN MACGREGOR

Maintenance was undertaken in the old locomotive sheds at Pennyburn, which dated from the earliest days of the railway, with 3ft gauge track defining the width of the inspection pits. Ex-Ribble, Saunders Roe-bodied Leyland Tiger Cub 112 (FCK 862) is in the shed on the right.

although actually then in prison in England, nearly shared my spelling of the clan name, and more confusingly still, had grown up not far from my parents' house in Glasgow. Phew.

Anyway, the PD3 surged forward, and the conductor, who was clearly well used to having his waybill ripped up by the troops, lifted the long seat by the door and triumphantly produced a copy. That was how crews kept the service running.

I duly made it to Pennyburn, courtesy of a lift on an LSR road tanker, where I met Ronnie Hamilton, who explained the difficulties that the company faced, and spoke of coming timetable rationalisation and the necessity to convert to one-man operation, as it was called then, to cut costs.

Vows to keep running

Despite the Troubles, and Derry was still reeling from the effects of Bloody Sunday of 1972, which had largely destroyed the Swilly's traffic in shoppers coming into the city from Donegal, he vowed that it would carry on as long as it could. "We're here to serve the people of the area we cover, despite all the difficulties we're currently facing," he told me.

He presented me with some Setright insert tickets as a souvenir, and left me to photograph around the yard, the highlight of which was the former railway repair shops, with buses standing over pits lined by 3ft gauge track rails, as though an engine might arrive at any minute.

There was a variety of buses to be seen around the yard, from our steed from Letterkenny, now going through the wash, to a CIÉ C-class Leopard on hire, to a variety of Atlanteans and other assorted secondhand vehicles from Scotland and England, and I snapped away happily with my Instamatic of those days, bought in penniless student days.

When it was time to get back to the city bus station, to catch the CIÉ Derry-Galway express service, to drop me off at Donegal Town, I checked into the office to let them know I was away. "Hold on a minute," said Mr Hamilton. "We have a bus going down to the station to take up service and I'll get the driver to take you down the Strand Road."

So, standing beside the driver on the platform of his 23-year-old Saunders Roe-bodied Leyland Royal Tiger, we were halfway down the busy Strand Road, chatting about life in general and the Lough Swilly in particular, when an armoured car shot past the bus and screeched to a stop in front of us.

What had I photographed?

Out poured six armed soldiers, who screamed at the driver to open the doors and dragged me off. "Why the **** were you taking pictures of our base?" one screamed in my face. "Identity. Now."

I took out my driving licence, with its Irish name and Glasgow address, and demanded I hand over my camera. It was then that I produced the letter from Mr Hamilton and managed, among the shouting, to say that I had been taking pictures of the buses and had permission to do so. It then dawned on me that the building over the road from the Swilly HQ was the Derry British Army HQ. I had failed to clock that.

Following some radio traffic, the squaddies calmed down, threw my camera back at me,

disappeared into their Saracen and drove off. The Swilly driver just shrugged. "It's like this for us all the time," he said. "You're lucky, though, you weren't arrested and taken away for internment." Imagine explaining that to the parents and the fiancée.

As luck would have it, I knew the driver of the Donegal-bound bus, who said he'd drop me off at Laghey, even though it wasn't a scheduled stop, and it was a relief to cross the border. Even the rough riding of the C bus didn't worry me too much. It was good not to be in the cells, under interrogation, just because I was a bus enthusiast.

What I had experienced, nearly 50 years ago, was what it was like to provide a bus service at one of the worst times in the history of Derry. But it was clear, even then, that a mortal blow had been dealt to the Swilly, which was finally to succumb in 2014.

It was probably a bit mad to go up to Derry as a young man in July 1974, but I did phone herself successfully, we got married the following year and are still going strong, saw the Swilly in action, and above all was kept out of jail by the official letterhead of the Londonderry & Lough Swilly Railway.

Not many bus fans can claim all that and the crucial letter still has pride of place in my collection of Lough Swilly bits and pieces. It is, after all, a get-out-of-jail free card. ■

Until 1967, Lough Swilly livery for most vehicles was green and grey, as applied to its first Leyland Atlantean, 87 (UI 8616) with Metro-Cammell body, which was acquired in 1960 and kept for 20 years. It was new in 1959 as a Leyland demonstrator registered 46 LTB. It was re-registered 8895 XI for evaluation in Belfast, then HZA 723 for trials in Dublin. Parked behind it in Buncrana in June 1968 is Duple-bodied Leyland Royal Tiger 104 (LUF 607), a coach acquired ex-Southdown in 1964 and withdrawn in 1974. IAIN MACGREGOR

Fond farewells

Over the years, **LAURENCE KNIGHT** has obsessed over several iconic buses, which then slipped away into retirement – their departure sometimes unnoticed. In a bout of unashamed nostalgia, he recalls several of these departing delights, and his memories surrounding them.

The summer of 1969, immortalised in song and, as a youthful bus spotter, the year that one of the harsh realities of life was impressed on me: like my parents' cats, buses did not last forever; you had to learn to love the new ones that took their place.

Northampton Corporation's five remaining 1950 Roe-bodied Daimler CVG6s were special with their varnished wood interiors, shiny chrome radiator shells and wonderfully melodious gearboxes that provided a soothing accompaniment to my reluctant journeys to junior school.

I did not even notice they were gone for some time – life went on as normal – then the grim realisation hit me. A visit to the back of St James'

depot confirmed my worst fears: there they were, lined up and lifeless, ghostly and toothless, as withdrawn buses often looked when stripped of their destination blinds and dulled by dust.

A fitter offered to sell me one for 5/- (25p). I was taken in by his merciless ruse, and glared at him malevolently a couple of months later as bus 186 (ANH 186) was jacked up by hard-bitten scrap men, substituting dirty old slave wheels for its shiny red ones. Its fate from that point onwards was a long journey up the M1 to the killing fields of Barnsley.

Fortunately, United Counties continued to provide entertainment with its handsome lowbridge Bristol KSWs. These were also on the way out, but Northampton was was also home to the company's central works. Sometimes a "foreign" KSW at the end of its life would come home for a few last weeks of service on my local route, then settle in a quiet corner with others behind the works, forgotten and forsaken. I would explore their musty interiors.

Remaining KSWs were restricted to town service, but exceptions added excitement to life. On one of those days when everything seems to go right, I emerged from a Christmas jumble sale at Northampton Town Hall clutching a cherished acquisition – my first Matchbox STL toy bus. Entering the fume-ridden depths of Derngate bus station, I encountered a KSW5G with unfamiliar TNO registration, due to depart to Wellingborough and Raunds. I paid my 2/- (10p) fare, and I was off on an unforgettable ride through the fog to Wellingborough – an excursion seemingly to the back of beyond to this 12-year-old (literally so, as we passed a pub in Ecton called The World's End).

The old K type puffed and grunted through

The last RT in normal service with London Transport, RT624, ran into Barking garage from route 62 at around midday on April 7, 1979. Not only did Mr Knight miss out on this, but also the ticket-only afternoon commemorative run. At least he could photograph the departure. Four exuberant enthusiasts lean out of the top deck of RT3251 — now preserved by Ensignbus — as it leaves Barking, where Austin 1100s, Ford Cortinas, flared trousers and long hair complete the 1970s tableau.

the rolling countryside with a standing load, rear wheels scuffing on wheelarches; finally, at Wellingborough, I watched its ghostly form fade away into the fog, its tungsten lights adding to the Dickensian atmosphere of Christmas. My first and last sighting of an ex-Eastern National K type.

Northampton Corporation's 1957 Birmingham-front CVG6s numbered 200-9 — which trundled alluringly past my school – became the next subject of my obsessions, but 20 single-deck Daimler Fleetlines arrived on Sunday April 8, 1973, sending Leyland 680 engine noises reverberating across the town, and swept the old tin fronts out of service. On their last afternoon, 201 was the only one that had not slunk back to the depot. I saw no other enthusiasts, so my near-empty ride back to town was a solitary experience, as our hobby so often is.

Adventures on RTs
Family trips to London revealed a more vibrant side to bus operations than in sleepy Northampton. Seeing bus types numbered in the thousands was overwhelming.

After constant haranguing, my parents finally allowed me to have a bus day in the capital, and as I stepped out of Euston station I was bewildered by the vast numbers of Routemasters urgently

Birmingham was a revelation, with many "Standard" Daimlers and Guys still in service. These two 1953 examples — Crossley-bodied Daimler CVG6 2832 (JOJ 832) and Guy Arab 2943 (JOJ 943) with Metro-Cammell body — wait time at the Hamstead terminus of lengthy cross-city route 15/16 in 1975. The apparent interloper behind the Guy is ex-West Bromwich CVG6-30 246H (246 NEA) with Metro-Cammell body, new in 1963. The Bundy clock to the left of 2832 was wound by the driver to ensure correct departure time.

going about their business. But my quarry was the rapidly-disappearing RT. On a Saturday the type passed Euston station at regular intervals on a cross-London route, the 77c to Raynes Park.

Three-mile trundles on Northampton's Daimlers had nothing on this epic voyage. Pressing ever onwards, passengers piling on and off, driver expertly executing changes up and down the preselector gearbox...we ploughed through the south-western London suburbs, until the cold hand of fear gripped me. How would I ever get back to Euston, and how long would it take?

I need not have worried. A pageant of RTs processed in the other direction, and armed with my Red Bus Rover, I hopped on and off at will to broaden my RT experience.

When I returned to London for a follow-up feast, I chose a weekday, and the world was my oyster – figuratively speaking, since Oyster cards were still 30 years in the future; in those days it was the Red Rover that got me cheaply all over London. Besides the 77 group, a plethora of other treats awaited.

For a real odyssey, the 109 – from Westminster to Purley, in Surrey – was awe-inspiring in both its length and the number of RTs employed (around 60, from several garages). A day could be spent on this route alone, but then there was the 1 from Trafalgar Square to Catford, the 47 that went far beyond this point to Farnborough in Kent; and in north-west London — looking quaint alongside the Boeing 747s

at Heathrow Airport — RTs could be seen on the marathon 140 to 'arrow on the 'ill and beyond.

But one disappointment after another lay in wait; my excursions were met with the depressingly familiar sight of RT routes in the hands of Routemasters or DMS Fleetlines. Entire enclaves were wiped out, even south of the river – where, unlike West End taxis, the RT had reigned supreme.

I flitted from one area to another in my pursuit of a fix, and ended up in Barking. RTs had become *persona non grata* in the Central Area, and acceptable enough though the 62 to Barkingside was, dreary suburban sprawl seemed a low-key climax to 40 years' operation of such an icon.

As the last RT day approached, the old girls were looking their age, with faded paintwork, worn and split seat cushions, and missing radiator badges and bonnet numbers. Cheerful adverts were pasted over with red paper, almost in an act of mourning.

Dreams of London Transport organising a farewell run through central London were not to be, and fate decreed that on the last day, April 7, 1979, I was denied a ride even on the humble 62.

The final journey was undertaken by RT624, nominally the oldest, but this last run was already over when I arrived. An afternoon procession of RTs along the 62 was ticket-only, and I felt singularly snubbed, but I had the last laugh over LT. No one could have got more value from a Red Bus Rover, or more RT rides, than I did.

Birmingham's Standards

Up and down the country, halfcab buses were rapidly disappearing, the process given a hearty kick up the rear entrance by government grants that halved the cost of a new bus.

So why would I visit Birmingham, swimming in a sea of Daimler Fleetlines? Because traditional ex-Birmingham City Transport Daimler CVG6s and Guy Arabs with straight-staircase bodies dating from 1950-54 were allegedly still around. Fond though I was of the RT, in 1973 I took my courage in one hand and my Cheapday ticket in the other, and took to the bustling streets of central Brum.

What a contrast to Northampton. Busy streets echoed to the roars of Fleetlines as they tore away from stops, barely after the last passengers had boarded. Convoys of them chased each other along flyovers and peeled off in all directions, and the general sense of urgency left this solitary young enthusiast distinctly bewildered.

Where were these bizarre destinations – Lozells, Bangham Pit, Great Barr, Shard End? How would I get back? What fury would erupt if I did not have the exact amount to drop in the farebox?

Feeling disconsolate, I dragged my feet back in the direction of New Street station, but then...there it was. An implausibly narrow-looking rear end, resembling a cream-painted London trolleybus, bounced along, keeping pace remarkably well with the Fleetlines. Stunned by the incongruity of something of a bygone age casually mingling with the modern traffic and concrete jungle, I rushed to locate a stop for route 6 to Bearwood. Impatience is not a virtue — a short wait seemed inordinately long — but finally, 1953 Crossley-bodied Daimler CVG6 2843 (JOJ 843) hove into view.

Its lower deck interior transported me to an earlier age — polished wood, chromium fittings and dark brown paint were all around, and a rich cocktail of hot oil and old leathercloth assaulted my nostrils. The time capsule swung round roundabouts and dived into underpasses, stopping only briefly for passengers to board or alight before accelerating sharply away, the driver roaring his way through the preselector gearbox. Here was a museum piece that was shown no mercy as a member of a big and busy city bus fleet.

What was striking was the everyday normality of it all, even more so when I upgraded from a Saturday to a weekday visit; well over 100 veterans perpetuating their own little time-warps on several

The future catches up with West Midlands Guy Arab/Metro-Cammell 2529 (JOJ 529) of 1950 in Corporation Street, Birmingham in 1975. Brand new Park Royal-bodied Daimler Fleetline 4612 (JOV 612P) is among those that have just replaced 1952 Daimler CVG6s on route 92. More will soon descend on the 15/16, the last crew-operated cross-city service.

routes. This included the legendary Outer Circle, a 2hr long, 25mile epic ride through contrasting environments — Europe's longest urban bus route. The Outer Circle became the final home for these "Standards", though seeking one out became harder as Metro-Cammell Orion-bodied Daimlers, surplus from Coventry and West Bromwich, began to steal their crown.

Right up to the end, 33 of them clung on tenaciously, even on odd peak hour trips from town tied in with Outer Circle schedules, but I never knew their last day would be Friday October 28, 1977. Once again I never got to say goodbye. Can you sense a theme developing?

November heralded one of the most depressing bus trips I have ever undertaken. Charmless Fleetlines – for this is how they seemed – delighted in whisking me to every vacated habitat of the old Standard. Birmingham — the same, and yet somehow not the same — suddenly seemed a dull and dreary place that I did not wish to revisit.

Lodekka love affair

During a prolonged period of mourning, I lost interest in the bus scene. However, five years previously, in United Counties' Kettering bus station, the seeds were sown as I listened in wonder to the gurglings of a Gardner five cylinder-engined Bristol Lodekka FS of Eastern Counties.

It seemed inconceivable that LFS113 (FAH 113C) could create the same sound as a United Counties KSW5G; however a lengthy ride to Peterborough not only convinced me of this but also that my sanity

Autumn 1981, and Eastern Counties Bristol Lodekka FS5G LFS112 (FAH 112C) is in the autumn of its life, pausing after the climb from Castle Meadow in Norwich. Maligned by many enthusiasts, National Bus Company poppy red could look quite pleasant if recently applied and in the right light. Some of the last rear-loaders had a reprieve in December 1981 because of a vehicle shortage, and LFS112 was one of them.

was in question. One and a half hours' throbbing vibration from its 5LW left me stirred but noticeably shaken, and a long wait in Peterborough's draughty, exposed old bus station added earache to headache — and a week off school.

Those FS5Gs seemed smarter than the FS6Bs of United Counties, and became my new best friends in years to come. Two cream bands, meticulously lined-out in black, cheerful cherry red paintwork, and – with a prevailing wind and not the slightest incline in sight – the engagement of overdrive fifth gear, opening up a whole new repertoire of rhythmic vibrations and whines. United Counties' four-speed Lodekkas on the other hand would grind along interminably at 38mph, chuffing away against the merciless governor of their Bristol engines.

A less than illustrious time at Northampton Grammar School led inexplicably to further education, and in autumn 1978 I was unpacking my suitcase in the fine city of Norwich, the heart of the Eastern Counties empire. It struck me as ironic that the operator chose the lesser powered FS5G because of the undemanding flat terrain of East Anglia, yet the city of Norwich itself was surprisingly hilly — even the bus station was on an incline — and it was here that many of the remaining ones were eking out their last days.

No distinguished Tilling red to be seen by now, but the FS5Gs contrived to look bright and cheerful in National Bus Company poppy red. Paint technology had moved on, and no longer did they seem to turn pink. My digs, atop a steep hill, overlooked Norwich, and with 40 FS5Gs on city service, inevitably one would sometimes haul me heavenwards towards my home in Heartease Estate in the evening rush. Passengers were not surprised to see cyclists overtaking the bus at the steepest part of Kett's Hill; I heard one say to the conductor: "No need to ring the bell, boy – aah'll jus' 'op off!."

Country routes were generally single-crewed, but there were benefits to lingering in Surrey Street bus station from late afternoon. Double crews were allocated to peak runs on what were known as "county" routes, and would take pot luck with what was left in the depths of Surrey Street garage. Sure enough, those Gardner 5LW throbs and barks would resonate against the walls as an FS5G left for some far-flung outpost in deepest Norfolk.

To the west it could be Wymondham and points beyond; this was my first adventure, immortalised in my memory by the hysterical mirth of the passengers when I asked for a return to "Why-mond-ham". The UK has a proud history of towns whose pronunciation defies logic, and

Eastern Counties' ECW-bodied Bristol MW5Gs provided great entertainment, running deep into the Norfolk countryside, but were often outstationed and could not be guaranteed to return to Norwich. No such problem with LM641 (KAH 641D) at Woodbastwick in 1979. This was one of two built to a standee layout, with centre exits (removed before entering service) and cove windows.

"Windham", as it is correctly intoned, is up there with Barnoldswick ("Barlick"), Norwich's Costessey ("Cozzy") and a couple from Northamptonshire that even challenge BBC local radio — Rothwell ("Roll"), and Cogenhoe ("Cook-no").

Weekend rides

I settled in my digs and applied myself diligently to my studies, determined to return some semblance of value to the taxpayers who funded me. Yet with spare time in my first year, the temptations of 60-odd red Lodekkas were all around. Armed with my £1.30 Anywhere ticket, a spring Saturday morning saw me lurking in the bus station, counting rivets on the Leyland National opposite.

Patience soon paid off; from deep within the Aladdin's Cave of the adjoining garage came the strident bark of a 5LW. Ushered out by a cloud of cold Gardner diesel fumes, LFS110 (ENG 110C) pulled on to the bay and we were off to Kenninghall.

I had no idea where it was, though at least I could pronounce it; over an hour later, we terminated at a quaint village in the Norfolk countryside, between Attleborough and Thetford. This ride was all the more memorable because LFS110 was blessed with a five-speed gearbox — and it displayed 'KENNINGHALL' rather than 'SERVICE'.

Small wonder that I never got stranded in the middle of nowhere on these "county" rides, but Lodekkas by now were not outstationed, so a

return to the Fine City was always on the cards. Not so, however, with the MW5G single-decker that busied its way back to Aylsham at 17:00, loaded with shoppers and workers returning home.

At the terminus, the bemused driver spotted me, blithely ensconced and ready for a return journey. "I'm going back to Naarwich now," I reassured him (the local dialect was rubbing off). But his riposte was spicy: "Not wi' me you'm not, oi's finish." There were no more departures that evening to Naarwich, MW or otherwise, so I indulged in a time-honoured student tradition...hitch-hiking.

Other memorable teatime treats included runs to Lowestoft, Great Yarmouth and Cromer. I often engaged with the crew at the terminus, although they probably regarded me with a degree of pity for not having a life, and I complimented one driver on the smoothness of his gearchanges. When I expressed disbelief that gears could be changed without using the clutch, I was invited to squeeze into the cab to witness the wizardry first-hand.

As the Lodekkas faded away, so did these nocturnal novelties. The FLFs maintained the tradition for a while longer, but remaining FS5Gs drifted to extinction in November 1981. For a while the city streets seemed eerily quiet, but arctic weather crippled the fleet and some were revived. I left Norwich in 1982 and never witnessed the end of its Lodekkas, but I did attend an earlier commemorative run.

Life goes on as normal by the markets in Birmingham in 1997, as enthusiasts bustle for a final Fleetline fix on their last day of service with Travel West Midlands. By happenstance, MCW-bodied Travel West Midlands 7000 (WDA 700T) — its highest-numbered Fleetline — carries the same number as the registration of the first ever Fleetline, 7000 HP, which was demonstrated in the city in 1960. That historic bus was lost in a depot fire in January 1976, though its rear numberplate survives on display at the Transport Museum Wythall, where Fleetline 7000 has been smartly restored.

Finding the Fleetline

Familiarity breeds contempt, which is probably why some buses were unpopular in their heyday. But over time, attitudes change, and I understand there are enthusiasts who, between therapy sessions, now get excited about Leyland Nationals.

My love for the asthmatic archetype of the 1970s has never flowered, but in a world almost bereft of halfcabs, the rear-engined Daimler/Leyland Fleetline of West Midlands PTE moved up the pecking order. Like earlier Daimlers, it had a Gardner engine and four-speed epicyclic gearbox. The whole ensemble — with its businesslike but handsome "Standard" body — seemed somehow just right, and quickly earned my affection.

On the other hand, I did not have to drive them. Crews found their cabs basic, steering heavy and suspension rough, whereas the incumbent MCW Metrobus had excellent power assistance and glided smoothly on air suspension over Birmingham's indifferent road surfaces.

Early Metrobuses fell foul of corrosion, leading to 50 Fleetlines being refurbished, repainted and reintroduced to some of their former stamping grounds. The language in the staff canteen at Walsall must have been ripe – "Surely one is not expected to pilot Fleetlines, having been divested of them these past ten years?"...or words to that effect.

Once again, Birmingham became the focus of my obsession. Daytripper ticket in hand, I travelled across the West Midlands, from Wolverhampton in the west to the "mystic east" of Coventry, and all points between. So ubiquitous were the 140 or so Fleetlines that on some visits I travelled on nothing else all day long.

By 1995, old age was catching up with them. A sympathetic fitter at Washwood Heath confided in me that the cost of keeping them on the road was causing concern. The speed of their annihilation in 1996/97 was alarming, and on November 1, 1997 the curtain fell on 93 years' association between the West Midlands and MCW-bodied

Daimlers. Survivors were approaching 20 years of age, an amazing feat in such a tough operating environment, and well in excess of the PTE's target of a 12-year life.

I was working in Cornwall then, but travelled up to pay my last respects. Travel West Midlands marked the passing of the Fleetline by operating route 27 with the type, and held an open day at their final home, Washwood Heath garage — also now part of history. I travelled on the last one in service, 7000 (WDA 700T), then watched it being towed into the garage by staff, in time-honoured tradition.

VR valedictory

Employment has taken me the length and breadth of the UK, and for many of the earlier years the unifying factor was the Bristol VR. For my most enduring memory, I shall rewind to a 1999 autumn day in Chester – city of Roman walls, amphitheatre, Tudor-style half-timber buildings...and some of the last VRs in service with Crosville Wales.

My job at the millionaires' playground of Rhyl was drawing to a close; time then for a final fling on the Crosville, in pursuit of VRs. The summer had been enlivened by these ageing visions in emerald, plying between Rhyl and Conwy, but VRs dwindled away as summer faded into autumn. My ride on

DVG522 (BMA 522W) from Chester to Wrexham was therefore a quite a surprise.

But this was merely the warm-up act. On arrival, with a frisson of excitement, I noticed DVG500 (YMB 500W), displaying route 94. A quick rub of the eyes and quicker consultation with the timetable, then – without a thought of how I was to return to Rhyl – I embarked on a 60mile odyssey from one side of Wales to the other, border town Wrexham in the east to Barmouth on the west coast.

The old VR forged steadily onwards through sunny autumn scenery, along the valley of the River Dee, round the side of Lake Bala – the brooding massifs of Snowdonia beyond. Tourists settled down with their backpacks, drifting off to sleep; a labrador curled up under the seat in front of me; and the high-pitched transmission whine soothed us with its soporific lullaby.

We reached Dolgellau in late afternoon. Should I stay on DVG500 to Barmouth? Or catch DVG530 that was about to set off for Tywyn, down the Cambrian coast? Common sense (and budget) prevailed, since I was in danger of not getting home to Rhyl that day. Dolgellau was thus journey's end.

Soon I was snoring soundly on an eastbound Dennis Dart...no need to count Leyland National rivets to get to sleep. ∎

Journey's end. The ECW-bodied Bristol VR leaving Wrexham on Crosville Wales's 60mile route 94 to Barmouth in October 1999 was an opportunity not to miss. But after a sunny autumn ride along the Dee and Mawddoch valleys and round Lake Bala on DVG500 (YMB 500W), it was time to bid farewell if there was any chance of getting home to Rhyl that evening. Also in this view of Eldon Square, Dolgellau is DVG530, bound for Tywyn.

The ECW-bodied Bristol double-decker waiting to depart from the Leadyard bus station in Darlington for Bishop Auckland typifies the complex amount of rebuilding and recycling that bus operators undertook in the years soon after World War Two. This is United BAL7 (GHN 839), a K6A new in 1946 with a utility-style body built by Strachans. Its replacement lowbridge body was built in 1949 and fitted originally on a 1935 Bristol GO5G, before reaching this chassis in 1955. Modernity stands behind in the form of a Bristol Lodekka bound for Redcar. BTC-owned United served an area from Northumberland to Yorkshire.

Spring in Northumbria

KEN CAMERON's photography from the late 1950s and early 1960s has accompanied the Fleet News Scotland section in BUSES since January 2020, but he also ventured farther afield to adjoining parts of England

On an Easter break from school in Edinburgh, a teenage Ken Cameron headed across the border in April 1958 in search of the buses then operating in Newcastle and Co. Durham.

This small selection of what he photographed reveals how many people routinely used buses then and some of the great variety to be found in British Transport Commission, The BET group and large and small municipal fleets in which few double-deckers had concealed radiators, and underfloor-engined single-deckers represented the height of modernity and technical sophistication.

The world would need to wait another five months to see the first production versions of Leyland's groundbreaking rear-engined Atlantean double-decker. ■

This was Northern General 1519 (CU 6319), a 1954 Guy Arab IV with Gardner 5LW engine and 58-seat Weymann Orion body, in Durham bus station in the BET company's dark red and cream. The exhortation to shop at Binns, a message displayed on company buses across the north of Britain, was for a chain of department stores which by 1934 had branches across north-east England and in Edinburgh, Carlisle and Dumfries. It was acquired by House of Fraser in 1953.

A typically large queue of passengers is standing on Croft Street in the city centre as Newcastle Corporation 74 (KVK 974) prepares to depart for Wallsend. This was one of 11 Daimler CVG6s new in June 1947 with 56-seat Roe bodies. They were followed in 1948 by 14 others with 55-seat Metro-Cammell bodies, all in the corporation's striking livery of yellow and cream. The double-decker behind is probably a green and cream Leyland Titan PD2/12 with Metro-Cammell Orion body from the Tyneside Omnibus Company, a subsidiary of Northern General.

Coaching
snapshot '72

Two hours of recording coach movements at the Leicester Forest East services on the M1 on a Saturday afternoon in August 1972 provided **MIKE GREENWOOD** with a memorable record of the UK coach industry of half a century ago

cannot now recall what my mindset was 50 years ago. Much water has passed under the bridge since then, but I was intrigued by some detailed notes I have which are in the form of a survey of coaches stopping or passing the M1 services at Leicester Forest East on some Saturdays in June and August 1972. First, let me give some background information from that time.

I lived in Leicester, so the location makes perfect sense and at the end of June 1972 I celebrated my 18th birthday. I was also just a couple of weeks away from starting what a lifelong transport-related career when I took up a junior office position at Leicester City Transport. The National Bus Company was also just starting to get to grips with the coaching side of its business.

I made my first visit to the services on Saturday June 17, 1972 and I recorded 110 vehicles between 12:30 and 16:00. I was there again a week later and this time 94 vehicles were recorded between 13:30 and 16:05. I took a break during July, but was back again on Saturdays August 5, 12 and 26, with recordings of 140, 77 and 62 vehicles respectively.

The summer 1972 issue of the coach guide was yet to receive the attention of the corporate marketing team as it wasn't until a year later, with the formation of National Travel, that a properly integrated nationwide express coach network took shape. However, United 1290 was already showing service number 201. Service numbers 200-399 were allocated to the North East area. THE BUS ARCHIVE

*My Zeiss Nettar camera together with the 11 negatives
I took on the day in question.*

BELOW: *The first of the three survey sheets I completed on
August 12, 1972 and typed details of the 77 coaches I saw.*

For my August visits, I concocted a printed "NBC
Coach Survey 1972" sheet, actually used to record
all coach, dual-purpose and bus sightings and not
just coaches of the NBC companies. It had specific
columns for the details I had recorded earlier in
my note book in June – fleetnumber (if applicable),
registration number, operator, chassis/body,
direction (northbound or southbound) and time.

Camera in hand

For this article I have looked in more detail at my
observations on Saturday August 12 because that
was the only occasion that I also took my camera
with me. Don't get too excited because at that time
I was using a Zeiss Nettar camera, which had a

Given the small number of shots available on the film, it now
seems odd that I took two photographs of the same coach.
Parked on the southbound side of the services there looks to be
more interesting machinery in the background of the shot on
the previous page, but United 1290 (NHN 790K) was brand new
and in the newly introduced NATIONAL white livery so may
have grabbed my attention. It was one of ten 45-seat Plaxton
Panorama Elite-bodied Bristol RELH6Gs of which 1286 and
1287 had been delivered in July 1972, with 1288-95 following in
August. They were among the first deliveries in the new white
livery which had been announced on April 1, 1972 by National
Bus Company chairman Freddie Wood as part of the overall
reshaping of NBC. Responsibility for the new coach organisation
came under the umbrella of the newly formed Central Activities
Group. The first repainted white coaches started appearing
in June that year. At first, it was a novelty but it went on to
ruthlessly destroy the classic coach liveries of the constituent
companies, and some may say also the loyalty of both staff and
customer. Most enthusiasts deplored it increasingly.

fold-out bellows lens and no automated exposure mechanism.

Furthermore the 120-size film only allowed 12 exposures and for whatever reason I rejected negative number ten of the twelve 2¼in square negatives from the film. I have also transcribed my patchy handwritten observations into a more comprehensive document aided by today's excellent Bus Lists on the Web website.

On the day in question I recorded 77 vehicles between 13:25 and 15:25 which makes that an average sighting of one vehicle every 90sec. However, it is likely that I missed some because some of my photographs are of coaches taking a break at the services which would mean that I was away from viewing the actual motorway.

Examining the observations has revealed some interesting findings. Leicester Forest East is about 100miles from London, 185miles from Newcastle and 100miles from Leeds. It also was the chosen comfort stop of United Automobile Services and Yorkshire-based coach operators. United's express service to London must have been heavily duplicated that day because I saw 24 of its coaches taking a break at the services in my 2hr window.

This included many of its ECW-bodied Bristol RELHs but also three brand new Plaxton-bodied RELHs and four of the 1971 delivery of ten impressive Plaxton Panorama Elite-bodied Bristol REMHs. United was the only English customer for the 12m REMH and those ten were its last new coaches delivered in olive green and cream livery.

I was a little puzzled with my sighting of a vehicle registered RXJ 128J to which I had recorded

the owner as WA – Apex. WA was, of course, Wallace Arnold but RXJ was not a Leeds allocated registration mark and who was Apex? On this occasion Bus Lists on the Web couldn't assist but former Wallace Arnold managing director Stephen Barber kindly came to my rescue.

Continental feeder

He told me that Wallace Arnold's continental coach tours were not overwhelmingly popular

The next coach to appear in my viewfinder was WLJ 575K. This was one of 15 Plaxton Panorama Elite-bodied Fords that made up Bournemouth-based Excelsior's 1972 intake. Ten of these were 49-seaters on R226 chassis but the coach photographed here was one of five 41-seat R192s.

Heading north on the M1 is East Kent's Plaxton Panorama Elite-bodied AEC Reliance 6U3ZR VJG 479J. It appears to be operating on service X21 with an almost full load, although a destination isn't shown. The M1 was a different animal 50 years ago, with little traffic and no central barrier. VJG appears to be manoeuvring into lane three, presumably to overtake slower moving traffic in front, which coaches were permitted to do until the 1980s. A bellows camera was not the best choice of equipment for trying to capture coaches travelling at high speeds.

but sufficient capacity was achieved by feeding in customers from other regions. This was achieved initially by using third party minicoach operators but in December 1969 Wallace Arnold acquired the business of N Thornton of Pudsey, trading as Apex Miniature Luxury Coaches.

Included in Wallace Arnold's 1971 fleet intake were three Ford Transits with Deansgate 12-seat minicoach bodies, registered RXJ 127-9J. They carried Manchester registrations because they were purchased direct from the Deansgate Sales Division of Williams Motor Co. (Manchester) Ltd.

I managed to identify most vehicles that went shooting by, only missing four. Of these, the ones owned by Yorkshire Traction, East Midland Motor Services and North Western will remain forever a mystery but at least the coach belonging to FC Wilde of Mitcham can be reduced to a choice of two, KYV 841K or KYV 842K, with these being the two rare Plaxton Panorama Elite II-bodied Seddon

Five minutes later another south coast-based coach was making its way north and appears to be taking part in a drag race with a car. Hants & Dorset 1027 (JEL 426E), a Bristol RESH6G with the unusual choice of a Duple Northern Commander II body, was on a holiday tour. It was one of a batch of four with just 32 seats. The short wheelbase RESH was the least common of all RE variants, with just 11 built.

Wallace Arnold's 1972 intake included 35 coaches with EUG-K registrations, of which 31 were Leyland Leopard PSU3s, three were Bedford VASs and the other was a solitary 12m AEC Reliance, EUG 473K. This just happened to be the coach that I photographed on the northbound side of the motorway services. Stephen Barber tells me it was the regular coach allocated to taking the continental tours to and from Dover. So it is likely that it made a rendezvous with Ford Transit minicoach RXJ 128J at the services. The Transit would then, most likely, take some of the passengers back to north-west England. Wallace Arnold supplemented its owned coaches with new ones hired from the Gomersal-based dealer, Stanley Hughes. Twelve of the EUG-K coaches were hired, including EUG 473K.

Pennine 6s that it had purchased in March 1972.

The oldest coach I saw was HHD 348 a Plaxton-bodied Leyland Leopard new to Yorkshire Woollen in May 1962 and with Hebble by August 1972. This just pipped Barton's 949, a Yeates-bodied AEC Reliance which was new in July 1962. An impressive 20% of the coaches I saw were K-registered. The

three Plaxton-bodied Bristol RELHs, owned by United, took the accolade of being the newest, having been delivered that month.

By coincidence I now live in Leicester Forest East so I may just spend a couple of hours coach spotting at the services on Saturday August 13, 2022 by way of comparison. I wonder how many coaches I will see. ∎

East Yorkshire 922 (BKH 922K) was one of five Leyland Leopard PSU3B/4Rs with Plaxton Elite Express II 49-seat coachwork new in May 1972. It was heading back home to Hull. It has two-piece driver-operated entrance doors, an indication that it had met the specification to qualify for a 25% New Bus Grant. Looking through the second nearside window of the coach, you can read a sign indicating that the motorway services were operated by Ross, the same company that produced fresh and frozen fish.

Wallace Arnold Leyland Leopard/Plaxton Panorama Elite RUB 363G, new in 1969, proclaims itself to be 'ON TOUR' as it heads north in the afternoon sunshine. Meanwhile a gaggle of cars heads south on the M1.

Back on the southbound side of the services is the coach which got my vote for the most glamorous destination on the day – the Italian Riviera. The registration of Sheffield United Tours AEC Reliance 2U3RA 381 (OWA 381E) reveals a change of appearance. New in March 1967, it was originally fitted with a Plaxton Panorama I 45-seat body but this was destroyed by fire while on a holiday tour of Ireland in June 1970. Plaxton replaced it with this Elite II body in July 1971. I am told that it was the only coach in the SUT fleet with the square-style fleetname on the front panel.

Dodging back to the northbound side of the services ,the last picture I took on the day was this one of United 1289 (NHN 789K), another of the brand new Plaxton-bodied Bristol RELH6Gs. The United fleetname, which can be seen above the front nearside wheel, was very small and underlined in grey. This was the style initially adopted for white-livered coaches before larger red names were used. It was heading back to Newcastle on service 205. In the background can be seen a 43-seat ECW-bodied RELH6G in the stylish olive green and cream United Auto livery. My notes suggest this is almost certain to be 1262 (NHN 962E), new in April 1967.

Two of the broad classes of route buses dominate this street scene in Floriana, the town adjoining Valletta. DBY 350 has a 1956 AEC Mercury chassis and a locally built Farrugia body built in 1965. Behind it, with a Leyland badge among its embellishment, is DBY 425, a Duple Dominant II-bodied Bedford YLQ new to Bostock of Congleton in 1978 and imported to Malta by 1985.

The **Maltese** swansong

JOHN YOUNG takes us back to the final years of Malta's characterful yellow route buses, his pictures confirming that no two of these customised and often radically rebuilt vehicles were entirely identical

I visited Malta five times between 2004 and 2010, a year before the end of its yellow route buses, which last ran on Saturday July 2, 2011. Arriva replaced them the next morning with a largely new fleet of low-floor vehicles in its familiar aquamarine and Cotswold stone.

The route buses in their warm and attractive livery of yellow, orange and white had become an icon of the island state and featured heavily on mugs, tea towels, models and other gifts aimed at the tourist market. They must have been among the world's most photographed buses.

There were 508 licences, with buses registered sequentially from DBY 300 to FBY 807 with seven gaps, giving a fleet of 501. There were approximately 400 owners, many of them owner drivers. The summer timetable required just over 300 vehicles per day. This allowed for vehicles out of use (a handful of them for several years), some used on other work such as schools hires and drivers' rest days. Some buses were quite elusive.

The 501 fell broadly into four categories. The most interesting and varied were the 160 that could be loosely categorised as "Maltese traditional". By this stage only penny numbers were bonneted examples. The oldest had chassis that predated World War Two. Some had chassis that originated in the UK, such as AEC Reliances from BET group companies.

Most had no passenger door; the entrance was simply an open gap in the body side with steps into the saloon. Where a passenger door was fitted, the only time you saw it closed was when a bus was parked out of service at a terminus. On many

The ex-London Transport AEC Swifts underwent various degrees of rebuilding. Marshall-bodied DBY 426, photographed at St Paul's Bay, was numbered SM15 when new in 1970 and always was a one-door bus. The biggest visual alteration was replacing its barrel-shaped windscreen with angled flat glass. Mechanical changes included a Cummins engine in place of its original AEC AH505.

of the traditional buses, the fare was paid to the driver in much the same way as it once was on a Bristol SC4LK in rural England or Wales, with the passenger entrance behind the front axle.

Buses were customised by their owners with unique badges, brightwork and embellishments. Some of the badges could be misleading and all self-respecting enthusiasts carried the latest copy of the *Malta Bus Handbook*, which was an excellent source of fleet information, enabling them to check exactly what they had photographed or were travelling on. It also included details of the significant coach and open-top tour bus fleets along with a detailed route map (infinitely better than anything available elsewhere) and network summary.

A quarter of the fleet (127 vehicles) were coaches imported from the UK, typically with Duple Dominant or Plaxton Elite bodies. Many were now fitted with bus seats and opening side windows. Most were Bedfords; YRQs outnumbered YLQs, but the share of bodywork was split equally. There were a handful of Fords and a solitary Plaxton-bodied AEC Reliance.

Ex-London Swifts

A further 82 buses (16% of the total) also originated from the UK and provided much interest and variety. Most numerous were 34 ex-London AEC Swifts, some virtually unaltered from their days in the capital but others totally rebuilt.

Bristol was represented by 14 LHs, all ex-National Bus Company apart from one new to Davies of Pencader. The NBC examples were new to Crosville (three), Hants & Dorset (five) and Western National (five). There was also one Plaxton Supreme-bodied LH coach.

There were five ex-Blackburn Leyland Tiger Cubs, all of which looked different in Malta, and two Willowbrook-bodied AEC Reliances new to Aberdare Urban District Council. Further Lancashire-related interest was offered by an unusual ex-Hyndburn Dennis Falcon. Like the Tiger Cubs, it had an East Lancs body.

There were three Leyland Leopards, two with Marshall bodies from Yorkshire Traction and

Tourists board DBY 448, a Chinese-built King Long XMQ6113GM new in 2003, in Rabat. The flamboyant vehicle behind it dates from 1962 and is EBY 565, a Maltese forward control chassis with Gauci body.

ECW-bodied Bristol LH6L EBY 544, new to Western National in 1974 as its 1611 (GDV 460N) and substantially unaltered since then, operating service 652 at Golden Bay.

ex-Maidstone & District and a Plaxton Derwent-bodied example new to West Yorkshire PTE. Of five Leyland Lynx, two came from Preston Bus and three from Travel West Midlands.

More recent types were two Alexander Dash-bodied Volvo B6s and three Dennis Lance SLF/Wright Pathfinders, which were among the first low-floor buses in London when new in 1994. One of these Lances still carried route 192 branding on its rear window from its latter days with UK North in Manchester.

The balance was made up of a small number of Bedfords and Fords – three with Duple Dominant bus bodies, a Plaxton Derwent II-bodied Bedford YRQ new as Hedingham Omnibuses D136 XVW and seven Marshall-bodied Bedfords new to Norfolk County Council (four) or the Atomic Weapons Establishment at Aldermaston (three).

Last were the 132 low-floor buses bought new in Malta, making up a further quarter of the fleet. Most were new from 2003 as part of a then planned fleet replacement.

Most common were the Chinese-built King Long

(76) and Turkish-built BMC Falcon 1100 (31).

Local coachbuilder Scarnif bodied seven MANs and solitary examples of Volvo B6BLE and B7RLE, while five other B7RLEs had Greek-built Saracakis bodies. There were three each of MCII from Macedonia and Solaris Valetta from Poland (Solaris mis-spelt of the name of island's capital, which correctly is Valletta).

Most common to British eyes were four Dennis Dart SLFs (two Plaxton Pointers and two East Lancs Spryte), the latter to a different build to UK examples, most notably with manual gearboxes, and a solitary Optare Excel. Although new as an automatic, the Excel was converted to manual transmission when rebuilt in 2005.

Drivers show pride
Detailed application of the livery varied, but it still projected a united image. Vehicle presentation was generally high, with proud drivers often cleaning and attending to them in the parking area adjacent to the Valletta terminal at the Triton fountain.

Timetable details were sketchy at best. If you were lucky, you might obtain a photocopied sheet offering a summary of sorts, either from a kiosk at a main terminal or from hotels' reception desks. This

Typical variety at the Valletta terminal. EBY 543 in the centre is a Plaxton Derwent-bodied Leyland Leopard PSU4C/4R new to West Yorkshire PTE in 1976 as 8524 (LUG 524P). DBY 451 is a Bedford YMQ with Plaxton Derwent II body new to Hedingham & District in 1987 as L136 (D136 XVW), while EBY 595 behind is a Duple Dominant bus-bodied Ford R1014 new in 1978 as Ford demonstrator COO 242T.

showed departure times from each terminal only, so this was of limited use if you were mid-route, particularly on a long route.

These often bore little resemblance to reality and additional trips were provided at busy times. Frequencies were such that it wasn't too much of an issue in any case. "Direct" routes omitted Valletta, providing other useful links; they were numbered in the 600s and charged premium fares.

Enthusiasts often gathered around the Valletta terminal, the hub of the network. This was a spotter's or photographer's dream, but a health and safety inspector's nightmare. Buses and pedestrians mingled at random, with the great variety of buses — moving and stationary — placed at all angles imaginable.

To travel on a route bus was an experience. What sort of bus would turn up at your stop? Where was it going? No destinations were shown, never mind the luxury of via points. Only route numbers, so if you had no prior network knowledge, you could ask the driver for reassurance.

On boarding, you either stated your destination or the fare, if you knew it. Particularly in the days of Maltese lira, there was a fairly flexible approach to change giving; so long as it was near enough, that seemed to work. Would you then find a vacant seat? Many buses were busy and some were seriously overloaded, especially after hotel breakfast times, returning from beaches at the end of the day or on journeys from the Gozo ferry at Cirkewwa.

I recall a journey on Ford V8 EBY 500 climbing up to Mellieha with a full standing load. Its speed gradually reduced to less than walking pace, before conking out altogether to loud cheers and much laughter. The driver simply restarted the engine and set off again in first gear.

Driven with gusto

And how would the driver perform? They drove their buses with gusto, making much use of their loud and musical air horns. They could sometimes seem rude or impatient and it was probably a good thing that most customers had little if any command of the Maltese language.

Once when I was on a busy bus heading out of St Julian's towards St Paul's Bay, the driver pulled up at the stop line at traffic signals that were on green for him, sounding his horn a couple of times.

That was because he was collecting a pre-ordered pasty from a takeaway kiosk alongside; this was hand delivered to him in his seat. The bus then pulled away, with much honking of horns and waving of hands, the driver then chomping his way through this meal as we made swift progress along the coast road.

Bus operation in Malta took some getting used to for those of us accustomed to British operating methods. The ownership model made it inherently inefficient. Several buses could be discovered at outer terminal points on extended layovers. Young boys were employed as ticket inspectors, so completely different from the established principle in the UK of progressing from driver to inspector.

Services started early but finished early too, typically around 22:00. If dining away from your hotel, there was no time to linger afterwards. I recall once catching the second to last bus back after an evening meal at Valletta waterfront. We walked up to the Triton fountain terminal to secure our seats. The bus was on the stand in good time with the engine ticking over. The dimly lit interior

filled up gradually and we left spot on time.

It doesn't rain much in Malta but when it does, it can be heavy and the drains cannot cope. Flood water would typically lap around the open doorway as buses waded their way through.

First day out

To give you a flavour of the variety of vehicles you might experience, let me take you back to my first day in Malta in 2004.

Venturing out from the hotel, I photographed DBY 308, an AEC Mercury with Tonna body, then took first trip out on DBY 372, a Ford ET7 with Casha bodywork, for the short trip from St Paul's Bay to Bugibba.

We then caught FBY 706, a Bedford YRQ/Plaxton Panorama Elite to St Julian's on direct route 627, continued to Sliema aboard Gauci-bodied Bedford OB DBY 329 on the 62, and returned to our base on Tonna-bodied Bedford EBY 560 on service 652.

I have to admit that we avoided the newer low-floor vehicles, but I was especially pleased to sample a former Crosville Bristol LH later in the week as well as some ex-London Swifts.

FBY 706 had been new to Grey-Green. It was always interesting to check where the coaches had started out in life, especially if they were

It's hard to believe at first glance, but FBY 787 is one of the five ex-Blackburn Leyland Tiger Cubs new in 1967 and imported in 1981. Maltese coachbuilder Scarnif rebuilt its East Lancs body in 2001 with Plaxton Paramount front dash. This picture was taken in Bugibba.

from fleets that I knew. Examples of these were Bedford YLQ/Dominant DBY 425 (*BTU 654S*) new to Bostock of Congleton, Bedford YRQ/Plaxton FBY 655 (*UNU 178K*) new to Hartle of Buxton, YRQ/Dominant DBY 323 (*NLG 105L*) new to Bullock of Cheadle and similar FBY 746 (*NMB 279L*) new to Godfrey Abbott of Sale.

Many and frequent

The bus stop at the end of the road at St Paul's Bay was well served with buses along the coast to St Julian's and Sliema, and via Mosta to Rabat and Valletta. Buses were many and frequent.

The lack of destination displays was a source of frustration to my now wife, but helpful to me as it allowed me to pick and choose which vehicle to select for our trip. Over time, she became wise to this practice and her knowledge of the bus network gradually improved. She also made clear that we would catch the first bus that came to the stop, regardless of what it was.

One Sunday, we planned to go to Sliema and St Julian's and assembled in good time at the bus stop in anticipation. This journey required a "direct" bus at a premium fare, by route 645 or 652. Either would do. I was also aware of a route 627 which also served Sliema and St Julian's, but that ran from Bugibba rather than St Paul's Bay.

Imagine my delight when the former West Yorkshire PTE Leopard roared into view, showing service number 427. This was clearly a mistake for 627, I told myself. Perhaps the 627 did call here after all. Anyway, it was too good to miss, so we boarded and paid the premium fare, but it wasn't going along the coast road at all.

The bus was full and we were standing, so it was hard to work out where we were going. I realised eventually that we were headed for Marsaxlokk, a fishing village a considerable distance away on the opposite side of the island. I broke the news gently, but all ended well as we discovered the popular Sunday fish market there, hence the heavy loading. We have since returned several times.

There were more surprise vehicular delights on trips from the same stop during our third visit, in 2008. FBY 661, a normal control Willys Six Model 265 with Brincat body to the water park on the coast road at Bahar-ic-Caghaq; a lengthy ride to the

One of the rules of identification of a route bus was not to assume that the makers' badges were other than decorative and to expect a vehicle to be even older than it looked. FBY 661, photographed at St Paul's Bay in 2008, is a case in point. The badging says Dodge, but it was an American-made Willys Six dating from 1933 and fitted with a Brincat body built in 1949.

Sunday market at Valletta on ex-Crosville Bristol LH EBY 520 (*OCA 626P*), and the only other normal control vehicle I was lucky enough to sample, immaculate (inside and out) EBY 537, a Fordson ET7 with Micallef body.

I satisfied my desire to sample REO Speedwagon DBY 368 one afternoon on that visit when it was operating Valletta waterfront circular service 198. A stand inspector was alongside, trying to generate custom, presumably from those returning to cruise ships. His sales pitch was that "this bus is over 50 years old". He was underselling it, as the chassis dated from 1938 and its Aquilina body was rebuilt by Sammut in 1955.

Every day a running day

A two-week holiday in August 2010 was our last in Malta before the end of the yellow buses. Knowing this, I made sure that we undertook as many rides as possible on a wide choice of vehicles, especially

John Young's memorable rides included one on EBY 546, a unique and noisy creation based on the chassis of a 1966 Leyland Beaver lorry imported in 1981. Its Grech body was completed in 1989. Behind it at the Valletta terminal is one of the 46 Turkish-built low-floor BMC Falcons.

the traditional fleet, each of which had a unique character.

Personal highlights during this swansong included a trip on rather noisy and smoky Indiana DBY 434 from Valletta to Senglea, and another on EBY 537, the immaculate normal control Fordson ET7, from Birkirkara to Floriana.

Other notable rides were on the raucous, rather square looking but not unattractive Grech-bodied Leyland Beaver EBY 546, Bedford YRQ/Duple Dominant DBY 323 new to Bullocks of Cheadle, an operator local to me back home, the ex-Davies Bros. Bristol LH, the ex-Richards Bros. Duple Dominant bus bodied-YRQ, a couple of Leyland Lynx and a smattering of ex-London Swifts, some of which were very melodious.

We sampled both Marshall-bodied Leyland Leopards. A trip from Mosta to Bugibba on ex-Yorkshire Traction EBY 479 (*NHE 10F*) was a step back in time, while we intercepted ex-Maidstone & District DBY 427 (*GKE 457L*) at Sliema for a climb up to the narrow streets around Paceville on service 62. Every day was like a running day.

Well-kept ex-Aberdare AEC Reliance DBY 300 (*TNY 495G*) had become a particular favourite

Young Maltese catch the sun as three of the Duple and Plaxton coaches imported secondhand from the UK manoeuvre at the Triton Fountain terminal. Plaxton Supreme-bodied EBY 609 was a Bedford YLQ new to Armstrong of Ebchester, Co. Durham in 1976 as SUP 436R.

and ended up being my last route bus ride. Its Willowbrook body was better presented than sister vehicle DBY 345 (*TNY 494G*). I caught it from Floriana on service 49 back to Bugibba. While I would sometimes break my journey to catch a different bus, this ride was so enjoyable I couldn't persuade myself to alight.

Malta today

In the ten years that have followed, Arriva has been and gone, along with its controversial fleet of articulated Mercedes-Benz Citaros from London. Most of the large King Long fleet bought in 2011 soldiers on with new Spanish-owned operator Alesa, but the Maltese roads have not been at all kind to them.

Today's smart fully accessible fleet may feature bus types unfamiliar on British soil, notably Otokars built in Turkey, some of which are called Kent which is the Turkish word for city, but it otherwise is representative of the modern day with full disabled access, LED destinations, air conditioning, electronic ticket machines, real-time displays at bus stops, contactless payments and the Tallinja app.

Bus travel in Malta has certainly turned a corner. Although the loss of the old fleet was much lamented by enthusiasts, locals — especially those with mobility issues or young children — no doubt welcomed the changes.

And Malta remains a pleasant place to enjoy a holiday. The Malta Bus Co-Op started tours with traditional buses in 2018; these are also available for hire. And it is still possible to sample a traditional Malta bus, as a tourist service has been introduced between Valletta, Sliema and St Julian's, using bonneted examples of the old fleet. ■

Buses & Bridges

TONY WILSON shows how bridges can enhance a well composed bus photograph — whether the vehicles are crossing a bridge, passing beneath one or are captured near a striking structure that adds to the scene

A cast iron bridge and an imposing building provided the backdrop for this Northern Counties-bodied Leyland Fleetline as it promenaded along the Scarborough seafront with Shoreline Suncruisers in June 1998. From its busy beginnings back in 1978, where with 29 similar vehicles it joined the Greater Manchester PTE fleet, it had since battled on Merseyside in a mini bus war and still bore the livery of GM Buses South's Birkenhead & District. The Grand Hotel is the imposing edifice, while the cast iron multi-span Spa Road bridge was opened in 1827, 40 years before the hotel.

During 1994, Volvo produced four prototypes of its fully low-floor B10L with bodywork built in Sweden by its Säffle subsidiary. Three were left-hand-drive vehicles with three doors, while the other was a dual-door right-hand-drive demonstrator for the UK, registered L459 JCK and first operated with Sheffield-based Mainline as its 403. From there it was evaluated by other companies, before it returned to Sheffield with Traction Group's Andrews Sheffield Omnibus fleet in 1999 fleet as its 2338. In the new owner's livery with the bold Super Low Floor branding, it competed with Mainline on several cross-city routes including the 76 to Low Edges. Note the different interpretation of that location; maybe the dot matrix display lacked enough space for a gap between the two words. I photographed it on the Wicker just north of the city centre after it had passed through the arches of the nearby abandoned Sheffield Victoria station on the old Woodhead Tunnel railway to Manchester, closed to passenger traffic in 1970.

The dismal weather conditions of August 2009 were surely brightened by the sight of a red double-decker bouncing and splashing its way up the approach road to Ribblehead railway station. The unmistakable structure of the viaduct that carries the Settle & Carlisle railway not far beneath the low clouds provided the background as Cumbria Classic Coaches AEC Regent III with East Lancs lowbridge bodywork reached the terminus of seasonal service 570 from Hawes. It retained its livery from the days it operated with Bamber Bridge Motor Services as its 4 (UTC 672).

London Buses' recently formed London Northern subsidiary acquired nine Scania N113DRB in July 1989 with single-door Alexander RH bodies, S1-9 (F421-9 GWG), specifically for the London Transport contract to operate route 263 (Barnet-Archway). Scania's Stuart Johnson dealership in Worksop had them registered in Sheffield. Upon privatisation in 1994, London Northern and the buses were acquired by MTL Holdings, which transferred all nine to Liverpool in early 1996. By 2000, they had moved en bloc to the Morley, West Yorkshire-based Black Prince company where they continued in registered local service for several years. This August 2002 view shows 424 (S4 as was) having emerged from beneath the main railway line in and out of Leeds, adorned in a bold allover advertisement for a tile and flooring specialist.

The small village of Baslow in Derbyshire contains a 10ft wide (3.04m in new money) bridge over the River Derwent that links it with the smaller hamlet of Bubnell. It has been crossed regularly by buses for many decades. In July 1996, Stagecoach East Midlands 432 (B632 DWF), a Leyland Tiger with Alexander P-type body, new in 1985 to East Midland Motor Services in National Bus Company days, was squeezing across on route 58 (Macclesfield-Buxton), extended here seasonally through to Chesterfield.

Great Yarmouth Corporation upgraded its fleet in 1964 with nine single-deckers and two double-deckers. The single-deckers were short-length AEC Reliances with Pennine Coachcraft bodies (numbers 81-6) and Roe-bodied Daimler Freelines 18-20. The double-deckers were Roe-bodied Leyland Atlanteans and this July 1975 picture shows 6 (AEX 26B) crossing the one and only road bridge in the town centre over the River Yare. The other Atlantean was numbered 5.

For a couple of summer seasons, Go-Ahead's Konectbus operated an open-top service in north Norfolk. This ran from Cromer along the A149 coast road to the Muckleburgh Military Collection west of Weybourne. The sole bus assigned to the service was 50 (R739 XRV), a Volvo Olympian with Northern Counties Palatine body new to Solent Blue Line, illustrated here in June 2014, emerging from beneath the bridge that carries the stock of the preserved North Norfolk Railway.

This former Portsmouth City Transport Alexander AL-bodied Leyland Atlantean, HOR 313N, was a long way from origins of 1975 when photographed in Barnsley in the heart of South Yorkshire. By August 1991 it was number 140 in the fleet of Shearings, a company better known for its coach holidays, but which diversified into bus operation in the years immediately after deregulation in 1986 and ran competing local services in this town. It was about to negotiate the level crossing over the Sheffield-Leeds railway line, before which it had ducked beneath a pedestrian and service road bridge in the town centre.

A lengthy and high footbridge provides the background for Go-Ahead London General's Plaxton Pointer-bodied Dennis Dart SLF LDP41 (P741 RYL) at Raynes Park railway station in the south-western suburbs during April 2003. I am led to believe that this structure still exists today. The bus by then was around seven years old and bore legend advertising its low-floor and wheelchair accessibility, something taken for granted nowadays.

Some take the view that no bus publication would be complete without at least one London Routemaster. This is mine. As it sparkled in the morning sunshine, RM2100 (ALM 100B) straddled the road bridge over the main railway line through the centre of Richmond during October of the long hot summer of 1976. Allocated to Norbiton (NB) garage, it here operated the lengthy route 65 through the west London suburbs from Ealing Broadway to Chessington Zoo.

The high and long railway viaduct in Stockport provided the backdrop for Stagecoach Manchester 5020 (GBU 20V), an MCW Metrobus new to Greater Manchester PTE and still in GMS Buses livery, in July 1997. The four tracks of railway line are well used by West Coast Main Line trains linking Manchester and other parts of north-west England with London and the south.

Not immediately obvious in this July 1977 view is a main road bridge across the harbour area in Weymouth. Western National 1751 (RTT 970), a 1955 ECW-bodied Bristol LS5G of this National Bus Company subsidiary, progressed its way on to the bridge when bound for the naval dockyard on the Isle of Portland. What cannot be seen beneath the bridge is the railway track that ran along the roadway beside the harbour; this was used by goods and passenger trains to link the main line station with the terminal for the ferries to the Channel Islands.

Ground support for Air Tattoo

A First West of England Volvo B7LA bendybus passing behind a Japanese Kawasaki C-2 transport aircraft.

SHOLTO THOMAS explains why so many buses and coaches can be found over three days each summer at a major international air show in rural Gloucestershire

Air displays may be the main attraction at what many regard as the world's greatest air show, but the Royal International Air Tattoo (RIAT) at RAF Fairford in Gloucestershire also is a place to see the large numbers of buses and coaches that bring visitors

Relaxing Stagecoach drivers and supervisors watch the manoeuvres of a Chinook helicopter beyond a line of Alexander Dennis Enviro400-bodied Scania N230UDs.

and families of participants from far and wide.

The show began at North Weald in Essex in 1971 and moved to Greenham Common in Berkshire before settling at Fairford — around 10miles north of Swindon — in 1985. It was named International Air Tattoo in 1976 and was granted the Royal prefix 20 years later.

It was held in July on alternate years until it became an annual event in 1993 (the 2000 and 2001 shows were at RAF Cottesmore near Peterborough), but because of the Covid-19 pandemic there was no show in 2020 or 2021. These pictures were taken in July 2018 when over 300 aircraft from 30 nations attended the three-day tattoo.

The airfield at Fairford, no longer used by the RAF as an active base, has an east-west runway over 2miles long. There's a parallel taxiway with parking areas on which UK and visiting aircraft are displayed, together with refreshment facilities and enthusiasts' stalls.

A display routine was provided by the Frecci Tricolori, the Italian equivalent of the Red Arrows. Appropriately their national colours were trailed during their acrobatics. These Stagecoach Gold-liveried Scania N230UDs had arrived on excursions from Gloucester and Cheltenham.

Aircraft enthusiasts and the families of aircrews arrive in coaches from all over the UK and Europe. The coach park is nearest the entrance, a pleasant change from some other events.

Shuttle services
Since the airfield is somewhat off the beaten track, Stagecoach West operates a shuttle service, with double-deckers, from Swindon bus station. Many passengers arrive by train, the railway station being just 300m away from the bus station.

The police have extensive and enforced traffic management measures in place near the airfield, which include the use of minor roads for the exclusive use of buses and coaches, plus residents. Seven Alexander Dennis Enviro400 MMCs were

The number of special events in its calendar justifies Stagecoach West's decision to maintain a small reserve fleet of ALX400-bodied Tridents. Still carrying advertising from the Cheltenham Races event that spring were 17729 (MK02 EGY) and 18090 (VX04 GHY). Alexander-bodied Dennis 17729 was one of a large batch of Tridents first used for the 2002 Commonwealth Games in Manchester, while TransBus-built 18090 came from a fleet of ten which reintroduced double-deckers on Cheltenham-Gloucester service 94 in 2004.

borrowed from Stagecoach Manchester to assist on this shuttle in 2018.

Stagecoach West also ran excursions that year from Gloucester and Cheltenham using Scania double-deckers. These parked with the Swindon shuttle buses to economise on supervision and minimise the possibility of return passengers heading for the wrong buses.

To see all aircraft involves walking around 5miles, but First West of England provides an internal bus service with frequent stops to take visitors round the site. This is operated mainly from its Bath

First Hampshire & Dorset open-top 32033 (W803 EOW), an Alexander ALX400-bodied Volvo B7TL in Jurassic Coaster livery, operated on the airside service and provided the perfect mobile grandstand for photographing the exhibits above the heads of visitors. The driver found an appropriate destination on the screen list.

Barnes of Swindon brought visitors in these two tri-axle Volvo B9TLs. East Lancs Myllennium Nordic OU05 AVY was previously with Weavaway of Newbury, while Optare Olympus-bodied PN10 TOA was new to Birmingham International Coaches.

depot, but using its own staff from other depots, together with contributions from First Hampshire & Dorset.

Most foreign aircrews are billeted at hotels in a wide surrounding area, high-security transport directly airside being provided by Stagecoach West's Swindon depot together with selected high-quality coach operators. These vehicles are parked airside, well away from the general public. Drivers on this operation, together with the First and Stagecoach shuttle services, require advance security clearance. ■

First West of England 10175 (WX55 HWA), a Wright Eclipse Fusion-bodied Volvo B7LA bendybus from the Unibus student service fleet in Bath, picking up beside an RAF Hawk and an ex-Swiss Air Force Hawker Hunter, now with the Hawker Hunter Association at RAF Scampton, north of Lincoln.

Constantly busy on this hot weekend was The Beer Bus, ex-Portsmouth Corporation Weymann-bodied Leyland Tiger Cub TTP 992.

MetroBus days

JOHN WHITEING took this selection of pictures of the West Yorkshire PTE fleet between 1976 and 1981, when the purchasing decisions of constituent municipal and acquired independent fleets were particularly apparent

The West Yorkshire Passenger Transport Executive (WYPTE), which operated as MetroBus, came into being on April 1, 1974 as a result of the Local Government Act of 1972 which created the Metropolitan County of West Yorkshire.

The operations combined the former municipal bus undertakings of Bradford, Halifax (with the related Calderdale Joint Omnibus Committee — JOC), Huddersfield and Leeds and during the following years also took over the bus and coach operations of several smaller operators within its area. The erstwhile municipal operations each had greatly differing requirements and, consequently, vehicular needs.

While Bradford was primarily a double-deck and urban/suburban operation, Leeds had

Parked in Leeds Central Bus Station on July 11, 1978 is one of Leeds City Transport's first ten Leyland Atlanteans, Weymann-bodied PDR1/1 335 (CUB 335C). The city's vehicle registration office did not issue suffix registrations until year C in 1965, this being one of the first so-registered in the fleet. Shortly afterwards, Leeds adopted the dual-doorway, long-wheelbase configuration for double-deckers with some fervour, on both Atlantean and Fleetline chassis.

Leyland Leopards 3235 (PJX 235) and 3007 (UJX 917M) on the parking area above Crossfield bus station in Halifax on March 23, 1977; 3235 is an L1 model from 1962 with Weymann body and 3007 a PSU4B/2R from 1974 with a Plaxton Derwent body, delivered days before the PTE took over. MetroBus rarely used Halifax's exemplary destination display to its full potential.

followed the London route during the middle to later 1960s and purchased a significant number of single-deckers, always referred to as "saloons" in Yorkshire, to operate its newly-introduced Fastaway limited stop services.

Both Halifax, which embraced the former Todmorden and Hebble services in Calderdale, and

A 1964 Daimler CVG6LX with forward-entrance Roe bodywork, 4111 (DCX 111B), still carried its Huddersfield Corporation (post-JOC) livery as it climbed High Street in the town during the late afternoon of May 25, 1977, although its PTE fleetnumber was applied by the addition of a (slightly smaller) 4 to its existing 111. This bus was never repainted into MetroBus livery. It was operating to Longwood, although not displaying its route number (40). Several routes to the upper Holme Valley involved a reversal at the outer terminus requiring the use of conductors until amended in the early 1980s.

Here was a bus owned by two PTEs within six years. Park Royal-bodied Leyland Panther Cub ANF 161B, among West Riding vehicles in Wakefield bus station on July 11, 1978, was the first example built and came with WYPTE's acquisition on April 25, 1977 of United Services, which until three weeks earlier had been a cooperative of Cooper Brothers and WR & P Bingley. Its principal service was Wakefield-Hemsworth-South Elmsall-Doncaster, in part of West Yorkshire where the PTE previously had no presence. ANF 161B was new to Manchester Corporation in 1964 but Cooper's acquired it from Selnec PTE in 1971.

Huddersfield served large tracts of primarily rural territory and had consequently always had a large proportion of single-deckers in their fleets. These distinctions continued into PTE days and were later to become exaggerated as the trend towards the urban and suburban operation of single-deckers was accelerated.

The PTE established Bradford, Calderdale, Kirklees and Leeds districts based on the four previous municipal operations; After a few experiments, a livery of Verona green and buttermilk was adopted, with a curious angled band around the destination indicator which swept down 90° to waist level at the sides.

The fleetname Metro was used, followed by the district name, e.g. Metro Kirklees. From 1977 the fleetname became MetroBus and the angled band was phased out; the layout of the colours was also modified so that the green skirt was extended upwards over the entire lower panels while single-

deckers lost their previously green roofs.

It took several years to standardise the fleet, although this was never fully achieved before deregulation on October 26, 1986 when the PTE's bus operations passed to arm's length company Yorkshire Rider.

It was during these interesting years that I found myself relocated to Huddersfield. The ever-changing scene of the epoch is, I hope, captured in these few photographs. I will freely admit that, geographically, my choice of location was circumscribed by circumstances at the time and was biased towards the west of the area, particularly Huddersfield and Halifax but then, in my opinion, that is where most of the more interesting vehicles were located.

As Bob Dylan famously wailed, The Times They Are A-Changin'. Well, plus ça change, plus c'est la meme chose (the more things change, the more they stay the same). ∎

Former Huddersfield Corporation 4034 (UCX 234H), in the town's bus station on May 12, 1980, was a ten-year-old Seddon Pennine RU with Pennine Coachcraft body. Pennine was owned by Seddon. Huddersfield passed 21 RUs to the PTE with two further examples on order which appeared after the takeover and with Plaxton Derwent bodies, to which the PTE added three Plaxton-bodied examples acquired from Calderdale. The initial deliveries of these vehicles, including this one, were to dual-door configuration, but following serious bodywork problems they were returned to their builder and re-configured as single-door machines with additional seats. Huddersfield operations included rural routes over indifferent roads with unpredictable cambers, particularly at junctions, so to counter this the front panels on these vehicles were built to a raised profile to save the time and expense of repeated repairs.

Former Leeds City Transport Park Royal-bodied Daimler Fleetline SRG6LXB 1211 (UNW 211H), one of 30 new in 1970, in the Central Bus Station on August 15, 1977 between duties on service 42 to Harehills. This was one of the large fleet of single-deckers (all the others were AEC Swifts with horizontal engines) purchased between 1966 and 1971 for the Fastaway services but here it is ekeing out an existence on local work.

The solitary Volvo Ailsa in the MetroBus fleet was 3480 (LUB 480P), a pre-production vehicle new in 1975, one of ten with Alexander bodies built for four PTEs. It was the only highbridge example with a rearward-ascending staircase. It was in Crossfield bus station, Halifax on July 3, 1977 and was based in Halifax. It was evaluated on the route between Halifax and Huddersfield via Elland and was sold to Derby City Transport (100) in 1981 where it joined others of the type.

BELOW: *The PTE's solitary Foden-NC with Northern Counties bodywork, Gardner engine and Allison transmission, 7250 (TUB 250R) was purchased in 1976 and allocated to Huddersfield for comparative trials with the Ailsa, intended to be on the shared route to Halifax. In fact, the Foden liked the comfort of the depot so much it hardly ever left home. This was one of its rare forays into the outside world, other than to rallies where it appeared as a "pet" vehicle, and appears here to be operating on service and with a conductor as it enters the bus station. The route number and destination display is, however, meaningless as no such combination then existed. Possibly, given the time of day and the presence of a conductor, it was pressed into use on a school service. It was passing engineering staff from Yorkshire Woollen District engaged on the recovery of Alexander-bodied Daimler Fleetline 689 (JHD 330J), which has a Scottish-style destination box.*

The first large order placed by the PTE was for Scania/MCW Metropolitans, with 95 delivered between 1975 and 1977, all allocated to the Bradford district. This was May 23, 1978 and 2649 (MNW 649P) was leaving Huddersfield bus station on service 364 to Bradford, which then was a joint service with West Yorkshire Road Car as successor of Hebble. Three ECW-bodied Bristol VRs of Yorkshire Traction and another appearance of Ailsa 3480 complete the scene.

BELOW: *Another one-off in the fleet was former Huddersfield Corporation Roe-bodied Daimler Fleetline, 4477 (KVH 477E), photographed in Huddersfield Market Place on May 19, 1981 while working a journey to Meltham via Helme. It came off the worst in a low bridge collision in 1974 and had the upper deck rebuilt by Willowbrook, producing this rather odd effect. In the background are the tower of St Peter's parish church and a branch of Barclays Bank; both still exist. The church flanked Lord Street, the former terminus of out-of-town buses operated by the likes of Yorkshire Traction and County Motors.*

This Royal Throne of Kings
The royal throne is Windsor Castle which forms the dramatic backdrop for Thames Valley's newly delivered Bristol LH6L 201 (RRX 992G). When received in 1968 they were 45-seaters but Thames Valley reduced them to 41. The early style of ECW bodywork did nothing for the looks of the first LHs. It gave them a scowling appearance as if trying to scare away what few passengers there were around in the affluent Thames Valley.

The company itself only had a few more years of life as at the beginning of 1972 saw itself and Aldershot & District combined to become the very made up name of Alder Valley. You can almost imagine the powers that be, sitting round the table in the boardroom, thick with the fog of cigarette smoke and empty coffee cups (or worse) at 03:00 when a slurred voice calls out: "Listen, I've got an idea!".

In the **Bard's** words

CHRIS DREW takes as his theme John of Gaunt's deathbed speech in William Shakespeare's *Richard II* for a selection of bus and coach scenes across England and part of Wales

This Sceptred Isle
Not an island, but the sort of aisle that comes with a till waiting at the end of it. The diamond set in a sapphire sea that is Bluewater. It's a shopping city built in the style of Gerry Anderson's Moon colonies from the days of Space 1999.
It's also a Mecca for transport enthusiasts because like a black hole, buses get bent towards it. It's built in a huge quarry and the journey in could be put forward as a possible entry for a new ride at Alton Towers. All the major players visit. There's a series of reserved roads and dedicated buses operating under the Fastrack banner. There are even red buses that reach there.
I could get there on my Transport for London Oyster card and we're talking nearly to Gravesend in Kent. The pull of gravity is even strong enough to deviate National Express coaches from of their given path. Like Stagecoach's 53012 (VU03 VVW), a Plaxton Paragon-bodied Volvo B12M trying to regain its usual road to Ramsgate.

This earth of Majesty

Majesty indeed, in the shape of a Regal III which was the final front-engined single-deck chassis supplied by AEC for use in the UK.

Introduced in 1947 as a one deck version of the so-called "provincial" Regent III, it helped a war torn industry through the changing period of the early 1950s when dimensions and exports were expanding and the replacement of worn out vehicles was a priority. It was also one of the many chassis from manufacturers which helped various size coach firms into life and give them a foothold in the rapidly growing tours and excursion markets.

When production finished in 1957, over 2,150 chassis had been built for the home market. But what is a chassis without a body? And as David Frost might have said, what a body. Duple's A-type frame was based on a 1939 design and tweaked a little after the war to produce a classic of its time. It was held in high regard as one of the best balanced designs of all the similar shapes that were appearing around that time.

When the engine moved under the floor on later chassis, it took several attempts to come anywhere near the looks. How I wish I could have taken this photograph for real, but this Grey Cars coach was built three years before I was born. I had to rely on road runs from museums like Winkleigh in Devon to show me the proud majesty of a Regal on the road. LTA 629 is not only a credit to its owner but also a credit to the British transport industry.

This seat of Mars

A seat here would have been used to see Mars, Jupiter and the rest of the solar system. The Planetarium found on the Euston Road in London, near Baker Street station, holds any number of seats for you to gaze skywards and see the stars and in doing so travel back through millions of light years to the time of the Big Bang.

London Transport Leyland Fleetline DMS2563, manufactured near the end of production of these 1970s double-deckers, was passing the copper dome while trying to reach the route 18 terminus point at the back of the aforementioned station.

This other Eden

The Eden Project in Cornwall would seem to be one of the biggest gambles taken in the county for many a year but, it has paid off. These biomes were set up to show the public just what will be lost if we keep on interfering with the balance of the planet.

For those who have not been to see it yet, I can only recommend that you go one day, Covid willing. It's an infectious place, one that you want to return to over the years to see how it matures. It's divided into several distinct areas where the temperature and humidity are set to temperate, tropical and desert conditions to encourage the growth of the appropriate plant life. The inference is that we should leave well alone and let the rain forests get on with what they do best.

The paradox is that the public to be educated arrive at the Eden Project in their thousands each day, in cars, which are considered to be one of the prime causes of greenhouse gases. These cars often jam the roads for miles in all directions.

There are bus services. The first time I went there, Truronian supplied accessible Dennis Darts from nearby towns, but the most any car passenger sees of a bus is the free service that transfers them from the entrance of the project to car parks away up on the hillside, operated here by a Wright-bodied something.

▲ Demi-paradise

What a delightful scene. Ponies waiting for a canter cross the fields, two large butterflies have settled on our quaint little village bus. It could be straight out of Postman Pat but it's not.

At the back end of 1977 and in its death throes before it changed its name, Western Welsh took delivery of four Leyland 440EAs with Asco Clubman 20-seat dual purpose bodies. This style of minibus was just beginning to make operators wonder whether the personal touch would work.

They were painted into an attractive yellow and green livery, lettered Village Bus and a butterfly logo denoted their role on special rural services. They linked areas in the Vale of Glamorgan with Cowbridge, where this photograph of MD1277 (SKG 981S) was taken, with Llantwit and Bridgend.

▼ This fortress built by Nature herself.

Once, this area and the road that ran through it could spell death for many a vehicle. The road was the A6, and the area was Shap Fell. The summit of Shap is recorded at 1,350ft above sea level and has tested many a driver and machine.

Nowadays there is a memorial in a layby on the summit. It is inscribed TO THE DRIVERS AND CREWS OF VEHICLES THAT MADE POSSIBLE THE SOCIAL AND COMMERCIAL LINKS BETWEEN NORTH AND SOUTH ON THE OLD AND DIFFICULT ROUTE OVER SHAP FELL.

It's been much easier since the M6 was built. The hills are hardly noticeable and coaches like this unidentified National Express Plaxton Expressliner thunder across the roof of Cumbria without a second thought. Shap Fell is no longer the fortress it once was.

Against infection and the hand of war.

They are both here. The vehicle registered 48 AC 83 was one of a fleet used by the Royal Air Force to take personnel to and from events where they were needed. On this particular day, the Central Band of the RAF was playing in Westminster Abbey in London.

These buses tended to not carry any manufacturers' badges but I understood it was a Leyland Tiger with bodywork by Marshall whose roofline was reminiscent of the Bedford VALs owned by North Western Road Car Company in the 1960s to work under the Dunham Massey canal bridge.

In times of crisis, the seats could be removed and replaced by stretchers and the vehicles used as ambulances, with the assistance of the double doors fitted in the rear. After terrorist activities took place on mainland UK, it was decided not to give the forces buses identification marking which would make them easy targets.

This happy breed of men.

I wonder if the driver managed to explain this problem to the inspector when he arrived 15min late at Worthing.

Whether, as a Morris dancer, you come from Bampton or Upton-upon-Severn, dance Longborough or Fieldtown, or even believe in Border or the north-west clog, there is an anarchical streak which says holding up traffic is a given right. Often at a country pub, there is only the road to dance on, and at these times there is always a couple of minders with pints in hand ready to lay down their lives to protect the dance.

The Southdown driver of ECW-bodied Daimler Fleetline 393 (XUF 393K) can do nothing about it except complain to the police later, by which time the dancers will be sat at the back of a pub, having a session.

This little world

They don't come much smaller than this. A novel but effective way of filling in the gaps in the transport service in rural areas. Having had personal experience of these Commer three quarter tonners, I find it hard to explain why these van-derived minibuses were used. I found it unreliable, noisy and the journey for passengers was a cross between a white knuckle fairground ride and a mystery tour, seeing parts of the countryside not normally on the agenda of any other bus operator. Notwithstanding, better vehicles did arrive on the scene, like the Sherpa and even Morris Marina. Royal Mail Post Bus JRG 132P was fighting the terrain and a torrential downpour in Rothbury, Northumberland.

This precious stone set in a silver sea

A silver sea of glass and it forms the central attraction of Kew Gardens, surely a precious gem to the west of London.

At a time when Londoners were losing their Routemasters in favour of, in many cases, bendybuses, Kew had its own. The tractor based on a very short wheelbase Ford Transit which pulled up to three trailers full of, shall we say, the slightly elder portion of visitors to all far flung corners of the gardens. It's named the Kew Explorer.

Which serves it in the office of a wall

Photo opportunities like this don't drop into your lap very often. Walking back to work in central London, I turned the corner off Victoria Street and was confronted by STL441, a 1934 AEC Regent with London Transport bodywork belonging to Cobham Bus Museum parked outside the offices, indeed the then head offices of London Transport.

These offices tower high over St James's Park station and serve very well as a sheer wall, showing how important a position London Transport held in the scheme of things in the 1930s. Needless to say, as I was unlikely to see this again too soon, half a film was rattled off in the few minutes it was there.

Or as a moat defensive to a house

Something not seen much these days is a horse bus service. This one runs between Bodiam station on the Kent & East Sussex Railway and the castle itself. It saves a walk of about a mile and affords good views of the flood meadows which acted as a natural extra moat to the castle. It was crossing the single track bridge just before the castle grounds are reached. This bridge is also a good place to watch for barn owls in the late spring evenings when they're feeding young.

Against the envy of less happier lands

I can remember back in the late 1960s, travelling to my aunt and uncle's house in Bedfordshire on a regular basis. The last part of the journey to their village of Flitwick took us through Westoning which was the home of Seamarks Coaches.

At times one would glimpse a bright shiny Mercedes-Benz O302 coach in front of the garage as we flashed past. They had large stainless steel panels much like Greyhound coaches in the United States. Was this the threatened invasion we had all been warned about? Other foreign manufacturers were beginning to arrive on our shores with exotic new coaches. Volvo, Scania and DAF were being ordered by respected operators and it served as a wake-up call for the British industry. Some said it came too late.

As for Mercedes, the orders didn't go its way back then. There were some but only penny numbers in the big scheme of things and certainly no buses except for a couple for Selnec PTE as a trial. Things didn't get going till nearly 40 years later when orders for low-floor buses took off in a big way.

The three-pointed star can now be found in many a large conurbation. The Citaro, like 869 of the Oxford Bus Company, has seen Mercedes-Benz pick up orders across the board for rigid and articulated vehicles including in London.

This blessed plot

Two weeks a year, this part of south-west London goes crazy with backhand spin, net calls and shouts of "Come on Tim!" or whoever has taken his place. It has to be Wimbledon.

As far as my memory serves me, apart from special services operated during the two-week festival of thud and grunt, there's never been an ordinary scheduled bus route that passed the front door of the All England Club. Could this have been because, during the other 50 weeks of the year, nothing goes on or that fares are at a special premium rate during the fortnight and the ordinary fare undercuts this by a good amount?

The 493 is one of those invented routes, a name I give a route that has no foundation in history. It goes from Tooting (St George's Hospital) to Richmond, but not the bus station in Richmond itself but a small yard near a hypermarket on the Chertsey Road almost into Mortlake. It has, though, proved itself to be a useful route, giving much needed extra capacity into Wimbledon centre from the Tooting area plus being a link with Southfields and Roehampton with the large housing estates therein.

The through running from Roehampton to Richmond saves the usual change at the Red Rover. It was run at the time by Mitcham Belle, a slightly grubby-round-the-edges coach firm which I had known for years. It had a fleet of Dennis Dart SLFs to operate it with, either with Plaxton Pointer, or like HV52 WSY, Caetano Nimbus bodywork.

Sadly, things were not on a firm footing and many complaints were received from the public about the state, both mechanical and interior cleanliness, of its buses. Mitcham Belle folded only to be taken over in a blaze of glory by Centra, which also turned turtle within a couple of years. The route still survives in the hands of its third operator...at the time of writing.

This earth

Would that it was all like this: Cumberland Motor Services 262 (MRM 262F), an ECW-bodied Bristol RELL6L, ploughs a furrow southwards towards Penrith in the first few years under the ownership of the National Bus Company. The countryside speaks for itself.

This England

It was the summer of 2006. You guess something's going on when cars begin to sprout flags and white van man drives around
with a large red cross on the side of his vehicle. Now if it were rugby, I might understand it, but this was for football, a distantly related game.

Some bus companies got the fever and decided to join in. National Express did both with a coach with cleverly changed logo to read "Nation Expects" and some double-deckers which operated a free service to see the big television screens in Birmingham. Wilts & Dorset named 23 buses after the England football squad. In London, Blueways Guideline Coaches painted two Irizar Century-bodied Scanias into England's official sponsorship livery. W5 ENG was one of them. How did we do? Does anybody remember?

This realm

Woman's Realm to be exact. It was on sale in the shop of Owen Ladner behind Harvey's Albion Nimbus on the harbour front at Mousehole, Cornwall. Weymann-bodied RJX 250 was quite the famous little bus. Acquired from Halifax Joint Omnibus Committee, it was ideal to operate on the service between the town and Penzance run jointly with Western National which had its own small Bristol SUSs, also with Albion engines.

Of these three double-deckers transporting schoolkids down from Romsey Road establishments to the Broadway, Winchester in 1971 or thereabouts, the King Alfred AEC Renown, at an alarming angle on the camber of the dropping-off stop in City Road, is flanked by one of the company's Roe-bodied Leyland Atlanteans and a Hants & Dorset Bristol Lodekka FLF. Visions like this could be seen only on "schools" timetables. Remarkably, the AEC and Leyland survive in the care of the Friends of King Alfred Buses. The buildings on that side of the street, including that housing a retailer specialising in baby carriages, have all been replaced.

To the **Power** of **Three**

Half a century after entertaining this annual's readers for the first time with memorable words and creative photographs of buses in France, **ROBERT E JOWITT** takes a number as his theme for this characteristic recollection of buses and trams (and girls) he has admired at home and abroad over several decades

Fifty years calls for comment. I started half a century ago on *Buses Annual 1972* and am almost the last of the original contributors still with pen in hand.

Our new editor seems pleased that I should offer him what he has described in the past as my off-the-wall style, so I hope he and our readers can accept my usual digressions. And the fact that some of the accompanying photographs have appeared in these pages or elsewhere before now, but while connected with the theme I have elected to follow, they present a sample of my artistic predilections, some doubtless published before some of our readers were born. Other photos may never have seen the light of day. I have editorial support for this strategy.

Rather than dwell on the number 50, I will indulge myself in the subject of three…trio…three jolly boys all in a row… three wise men. There is always a fascination about numbers and while there are only nine of them, they can and do multiply out in one way or another. Whatever the case, they are vital in the transport industry, as fleet numbers, route numbers, ticket numbers, numbers for crew members and so on.

While here counting, let me digress again. In my distant youth, my family was wont to listen to a BBC Light Programme entitled *Those Were the Days*. I suspect it spawned various dire offspring, but was in itself fairly harmless and, amid diverse old-time dances, it included hearty chorus songs, one of which ran (approximately) *Rum tum taddle um, old John Braddle-um, merry country lads are we!* The verses were sung in order from number one, and while I can no longer recall the subject of number three, I have it in my mind that number five stated *Old folks dies when they can't stay alive…* a notion with which recently I have become more preoccupied.

Still involved in this (at least to me) entrancing digression), I cannot recall what was number three in *One More River till Jordan!*. Was it the Ant the Bear and the Bumblebee who were boarding the Ark? Such songs were undoubtedly sung heartily if in slightly inebriated vein on board coaches with dorsal rear fins or halfcabs, at that date still plentiful…but only just.

King Alfred and the Spinners

I must, however, abandon this unlikely assembly of animalia to return to the pertinent question of route numbers; and, in view of the parameters of this essay, the route number 3. My local route in Winchester, in my teenage years, was King Alfred 3A, known in geographical terms as "the Stoney Lane bus". I have written of this previously, so must resist the temptation of further fond memory.

In Bournemouth, where I continued my education, there was a magnificent trolleybus system which added quite as much to my education as did the College of Art, but route 3 was a boring motorbus...actually a rather rare and decent MCW Leyland full-front double-decker, but being not a trolleybus, did not at the time seem desirable. Trolleybus route numbers started at 20, served by exceptionally splendid vehicles.

I will here add that I extended my trolleybus exploration to many of the trolleybus systems still then extant in Britain; in several of these, as in Bournemouth, three-axle vehicles abounded, for example London, Newcastle, Nottingham, Huddersfield, Glasgow...impressively vast and handsome. They certainly qualify for mention in a treatise on three in transport, but I have dealt with them before, so will not risk flooding my allotted space with further comment, and must eschew two-axle trolleybuses save to say that three in a huddle could look very fine. I will return to such

case in a moment, but it is time first for further musical digression.

It was in this period that — as one does when young — I was adding to my collection of records. This had originally been a family affair of an HMV wind-up plus a handful of 78rpms, a bit of G&S and Strauss etc; and then swollen by the likes of Bill Haley, Lonnie Donegan; then transmogrified to a Dansette and 45s; among the latter being the Spinners singing *Green Grow the Rushes Oh*.

Thanks to the 7in dimension, the song, which properly runs cumulatively to 12 verses, was cut short at eight. It was easy enough to learn the last four, if unlikely by now to find a dorsal fin under which to sing them; and never mind what the words meant. Some were obvious, 12 apostles, ten commandments, four gospel makers, but who were the nine bright shiners, or five for the cymbals – or symbols? – at your door?

This accumulation, known or not, was belted out at dashing pace until three, where slightly but dramatically it would slow down and, by whim of the singers, go up or down (or both) with the ri-hi-

Also from Winchester around 1971, a fine Weymann-bodied Southern Motorways Leyland Tiger Cub, on what is assumed to be a works contract, c1971, has just deposited two trios of ladies in the Broadway. Cast your eyes to the right, and the back of one of King Alfred's trio of Metro-Scanias is just in view. Those with an eye for British-made cars will identify the approaching Farina-designed Austin A40.

Little Old Ladies Passing By, to pluralise the words of Gracie Fields. These there were crossing the forecourt of Winchester bus station, with a Hants & Dorset Bristol VRs, this the famous YEL 1T new in 1978, at an inebriated angle in the depot behind.

hi-hi-hi-vals. But who were the rivals? I can hardly believe they were the coach services with price undercutting on routes to London before the Road Traffic Act; nor yet the comedy by Sheridan, though probably I have worked backstage on it, in theatre opposite the King Alfred depot where then the spirit if not much of the earthly reality of the Motor Services still lived.

Coming in threes

Disregarding the briefly draped Three Graces beloved of Victorian artists, or any digressing on those apes of see, hear, and speak no evil, I will harp, as promised, upon the particular charm of a trio of buses together, be they three sisters or three quite disparate. Wherein such charm? I do not know, and while admitting that any huddle of buses, five or six or more, is ever a splendid sight, three together have special allure. To catch this I have from thousands of my photographs over 60 years tried to find a few to mark the date.

Four buses together seem to me not so appealing. We have four apocalyptic horses, four winds. Why not four buses? Or more? I remember London trolleybuses coming in five or six on a surge, a case I did not understand then and am not too sure how well I understand it now. Equally or even more glorious was the spectacle of four and then another catching up, Lisbon trams every one at least 50 years old, swinging round the reverse curves of Belem. Almost dazed I caught the fifth. This was in 1976, and at that moment I had no thought of the power of three.

Retiring from a surfeit of digressions, I will now attack the question of three in the parts of a vehicle, as in tram or trolleybus or bus, divided, like Gaul, into three sections, by corrugated rubber joins, known by the French, graphically, as accordeons. I do not recall that I ever encountered such vernacular term in German or Italian, but the theory of articulation was to be encountered in such places.

It began, I believe, in Berlin and the USA in the 1920s, and 30-plus years on was spreading in Europe, not least by the aesthetically questionable but interesting practice of sewing two old trams together with part of a third tram as a joiner in the middle. Generally, this treatment did little or nothing to hide the age of the original trams, could in fact be said to render them in uncouth fashion appear even older, as for marvellous examples in Zaragoza, Spain.

In Brussels, on the other hand, they managed matters rather tidily, for while introducing a fleet of modern bogie cars attributed to the American PCC style they rebodied, in 1963, certain veteran four-wheelers in some imitation of this style, and took this treatment farther in stitching together two such cars with a central section, the net result fitting rather well into the 1960s modernisation picture.

This interesting venture was followed, though only some years later, by new-built PCC cars extended to two-parts, and finally in 1977 came the excellent 7900-series of three-part PCCs. These were still running 40 years later, but with the increasingly objection-worthy defect of narrow entrances and steep steps.

My youngest son and I were tram hopping round Brussels to celebrate his 21st birthday, admiring Art Nouveau and Jugendstil architecture and the wonderful museum of musical instruments housed in a beauteous building in such style; where I was particularly delighted with the serpent and the hurdy-gurdy and above all a concertina of a type employed in the Borinage coalfields, this being in two parts, the lower played by the feet. Admittedly this is not three parts, but it shows very good grounds for describing the joining bits of articulated buses as accordeon.

It was on this jaunt on a 7900, on arrival at our appointed stop, that my son leapt with agility to the ground and 'ere I had started to follow, the doors slammed and the tram moved on. My son had the nous to pursue the tram and meet me at the next stop, but the events caused me to reflect that tempus fugit.

Crossing the border and going back to the 1950s in Germany we find, apart from ill-matched marriages of two styles of car, constructors started, with typical national industrial zeal, to build brand new true three-part trams of thoroughly modern character. Dortmund, Duisburg, Dusseldorf, Frankfurt were some of them.

Swiss triples

Swiss cities followed suit. In 1961, three more-or-less identical trams appeared, two in Basel and one in Zürich. All three were of very modern if still Swiss appearance, and of course in three parts. Basel 601 and 602 lasted 30 years, but 601 then suffered such collision damage as to be counted beyond repair, and 602 was converted a couple of years later to a "party tram"; I wonder if it remains today.

Basel went no farther with this idea (of 1961, not party) until two-part updated versions of Swiss Standard trams which had been introduced while 601 died were spliced a decade later with a dropped-floor centre section, a device now de rigeur and quite probably legally necessary. I do not read Swiss legal documents; but I was not likely in this case to be caught by a closing door.

In Zürich, on the other hand, the style of the first three-part prototype (1801) was copied between 1966 and 1969 (with the only visible modification, one set of doors instead of two on the centre section) from numbers 1601 to 1690. They were known by the title Mirage, though I can see no connection between a solid Swiss tram and a desert lake which disappears as you draw near.

Moreover these sturdy trams were followed, literally it could be said, by three dozen sturdy three-parts sets identical to the Mirage save only that the front had no driving position and a headlight-less front-end more like a rear and, though motorised, could operate only when hauled by Mirage. The ventures were nicknamed "blind cows", more suitable certainly than a vanishing oasis. The visions survived well into the new century.

If I have wallowed at length in the joys of Basel and Zürich I cannot apologise, for they provide splendid examples of transport systems operating in three modes: tram, trolleybus and motorbus. My predilections were vastly for the first mode, slightly less for the second, and on the whole little for the third, but I was ever well aware of this triplication;

In Genoa, three Fiat trolleybuses face the competition, a dreadful ocean of bug-like Italian automobile traffic; this scene was in 1966, and it was likely to grow rapidly worse.

can I quote Glasgow, Liege, Porto among the classics in this category?

I have not yet dwelt upon trolleybuses in Basel or Zürich, the trams to my mind demanding all the attention I am allowed to give them. Trolleybuses in Basel were anyway somewhat peripheral to the tram scenario, and while I will not return thither in these paragraphs I must engage again in Zürich where they are in the thick of things.

Artics on three axles

First, however, I must touch upon articulated buses, in which many foreigners played a fine game in both trolleybuses and motorbuses. Such creatures, it must be said, were certainly on three axles – save for a few extravagant adventures into four – but with bodies of only two parts it is hard to say into which category they should be inserted. Whatever the spreading habits of Teutonic-speaking places, they did not catch on in well-mannered Great Britain.

Well, not for some time. Eventually – around 1980 – they started slinking in, in small numbers, to Sheffield, and, I believe, two of these migrated to Scotland. Some of these had a front in Leyland National style; I did not admire the back, either. Wherever else they appeared, including removing from Sheffield to other systems, they never seemed

to last very long or enjoy great success. I suppose I could admit them as continental eccentricities; on their own ground I quite fancied them.

Then suddenly, the first I knew of it around the turn of the century, certain routes sprouted in London. Here we had the Citaro, a not ill-looking machine, but appearing completely out of place among the double-deckers of the capital.

With feelings which were perhaps based more on politics than bus efficiency – though the Citaros were alleged, probably without much basis, to catch fire at the slightest provocation (even to the extent, dare I add, of being extinguished only by driving into Clapton Pond) – the introduction of artics by Red Ken was as promptly as possible scrapped by Boris and replaced by his New Routemasters, known initially as Borismasters, which, grand buses though they may well be, have little connection with number three.

Artics in Paris had appeared some time before, in the form of the Berliet PR180 which, while quite a presentable vehicle based on the replacement for the Berliet standard PR100, looked as out of place on the boulevards as did the Red Ken in Whitehall.

In the early 1990s I had once the pleasure of riding on an ex-RATP PR180 on the shuttle service from the Dieppe ferry port to what in the old days had been the packet-boat arrival, railway on the quay

In Vienna in 1963 we have a trio of these monstrous Gräf & Stift three-axle double-deckers which were introduced, so myth or legend or perhaps even history has it, to replace certain tramlines which were said to encumber narrow streets. Believe it or not as you will…

as at Weymouth, and later driving myself an ex-London Citaro, stuck for something like 12hr over half a dozen miles on a shuttle gridlocked for the Isle of Wight Festival.

All these experiences of articulation were firmly on two-part buses, though definitely on three axles. But in 1987 there came a most startling development, remarkably enough in Paris; this was the Renault Heuliez Megabus, an elongation of the above PR180 into three parts. (All Gaul). Its livery was white with a tricolour band flanking top and bottom and ends of the entire side.

I did not see this monstrous beast in Paris, for such a giant design and the dread Parisian traffic proved nothing but grounds for fairly instant divorce. I may add that ousted from Paris it enjoyed some years secondhand in Bordeaux where I must suppose conditions suited it better, but again despite my ardent wishes I failed to visit it.

Near two decades later I was in Luxembourg, and from my host's balcony was watching the intensive bus traffic towards the Rue de Thionville and southwards, as spotted through radial gaps between the buildings between the balcony and the road and, startled, started counting, and there briefly in the longest gap was definitely a three-part articulated.

Naturally I hunted up the matter, and continued in the art until recent times, while Luxembourg seemed to increase in enthusiasm for the theory... and practice. Luxembourg is an issue which, like surges, I have never entirely understood, for while a lot of urban services are operated by buses which by livery are those of the Luxembourg city operation, several other apparently urban lines are in the hands of suburban operators. The effort of disentangling what is what has always proved beyond my willingness to prosecute.

Of modern bus-like ilk

It has been sufficient simply to observe tripartite buses, in whatever livery may be present. That first specimen I encountered proved to be a bus of reasonable modern-bus-like ilk, except for the almost unbelievable rear, and the influx over several years retained elements of normal (if more) modern bus notion. Then others emerged with arch-streamlined bodies and such notions as wheels hidden away so as to acquire such ultra-modern tramcar effect that they looked wrong for not running on rails.

At the same time I included dashes to Switzerland, where, if the Mirage in Zürich was dissolving, there were three-part trolleybuses, known as Swisstrolley, effecting dramatic twisting gyrations among the trams, and then more of them in

Note that as long ago as 1959 Jowitt was engaging in the photographic possibilities of weather and architecture, here portrayed in Frankfurt am Main. The question here is whether a tram motor-car plus two trailers constitutes a trio, or do you need three trailers behind the motor-car? Most of the stock seen here are new postwar bodies on pre-1939 chassis rescued from under bombed-out bodywork, but the motor-car hauling the three trailers off to the right dates from before World War One. A parked unidentified coach adds to the atmosphere.

In Zürich this tramcar is either a Blind Cow or its towing master the Mirage. If the latter, the worthy gent in the foreground is perhaps quenching his thirst for fear the fountain disappears.

Lucerne and, I am told, in Geneva, while St Gallen, having built its own three-part trolleybus with disparate sections, was said to be heading for Swisstrolleys too.

If new trams were being introduced into Zürich, and various other places – to which we must cry "hooray" – they tended now to be in five or seven sections, absolutely spiffing but rather too mind-boggling for the lover of the traditional. Nevertheless, I feel there must be plenty as yet from former days to entertain me in Luxembourg or Switzerland for the foreseeable future...if indeed such destinations are attainable at all.

Architecture, TN4s and girls

Having reached this point in my narrative, I think I may allow myself to depart from the prevailing matter of three to indulge, given the time or date of this article, and this volume, into a few notes of autobiography even if risking a repetition (notorious bad habit of the elderly) of matters upon which I have dwelt in former years

I started on this transport photography — and writing, I suppose — lark more than 60 years ago in 1958 with a few photos, little better than record shots, of elderly German trams. By the following summer I was improving upon these with the addition of architectural background, weather, and citizenry, in Sheffield, Belgium and Holland...and more elderly German trams.

In 1960 I was utterly enchanted with the marvellous but fast-fading glories of Glasgow, trams between high tenements with the late summer sun still setting in magic light.

And then two defining moments. First, in Paris in July, I took my first photograph of a 1935 Renault TN4F bus, leading to a ten-year long course resolving eventually in my purchase of that very same bus and a subsequent 50-year career for better or worse as owner of same.

Then, a few weeks later (still in July 1960, in trolleybus-filled St Etienne, still in France) there were two girls in the knee-length fluffed-out skirts of the era coming towards me along the pavement, and a trolleybus – a choice Vetra – coming too, so I shot the ensemble. Thus was my photographic fate sealed, though I never neglected architecture or weather or various degrees of citizenry. It was thus that Gavin Booth requested from me a piece for the 1972 *Buses Annual*.

So for near a couple of decades – and from *Annual* to *Yearbook* and Stewart Brown editorial era – and then the powers that be (or rather were) in Ian Allan elected that they did not desire a Jowitt piece in the forthcoming *Yearbook*. I do not believe that decision was of Stewart's choice, but it annoyed me so much that I set up to publish my own work (under the house-name of my late dearly loved dog) and thus emerged *The Girl in the Street*.

I could equally have achieved *The Old Man in the Street* or *The Old Woman* or, for example, *Buses and Cattle*, but the girl might prove the most popular subject. It was a record of 30 years of ordinary fashions as were never seen in *Vogue* or *Honey* but simply as ordinary girls translated these to everyday wear, always with public transport in the picture. *The Sunday Times* reviewed it as "by some way the oddest book we have ever seen…"

IA powers relented in due time, and I was returned to the fold. And have been there nearly ever since. But by now *The Girl* was firmly attached to my name. I cannot deny that I find many girls attractive, and that many artists before me have delighted to render portraits of ladies, and if most of mine are spontaneous and therefore without the permission of the sitter — for a tram would be long gone and the final result might prove stuffily posed — there is surely nothing sinister about such shooting, merely genuine admiration.

In the same way (if not quite so much), I can admire old ladies or old gents…or cows or donkeys…or pigeons and rooks…and any quantity of any age of architecture, not to speak of trees or scenery.

However, there is a feeling in the air these days, rather like that which prevailed half a century ago on any sort of railway photography in Eastern Europe (not that I ever tried it myself, though I encountered it, if fortunately rarely, in propinquity to the Iron Curtain in Germany and Austria) lest it might trespass upon state secrets, only now it is seen as evil intention towards the human race. Furthermore, as photography falls into the digital art, I am too old a dog to be taught new tricks.

Less beauty to behold?

Besides all this – and perhaps another consequence of seniority – I find neither the girls nor the buses have the attraction they had in bygone days. Not that, for example, I ever found any great attraction in the Leyland National; it was a matter of compulsion, I just had to photograph whatever bus it might be, the more attractive the surroundings so much the better. In the same way I had to write of such travels.

A Zürich three-part-articulated Hess Swisstrolley 3 trolleybus and three-part trams in October 2009 close to the Limmat, which flows north-west from Lake Zürich near this point.

The buses now are hardly an improvement; the girls follow suit. It was I think in 2017 that I last saw a really lovely girl, she sitting at an open-air café table adjacent to that occupied by my party in Remich, Luxembourg, with a background of buses decorated with a huge motif of red Moselle grapes; but she had nothing, so far as I know, of association with number three.

Is it the case that the girls like the buses are less lovely? I recall in 1958 watching the girls descending the escalator in the Kaufhof in Dortmund where my host had bade me wait by the postcard stall (plenty of trams there to buy) while he went elsewhere; but if I were to see them again today would I find them all as beautiful and adorable?

I must be content with that which has been these past eight years my local bus route, number 3 from the depressing oft-boarded-up shops of the streets of the Isle of Wight capital Newport and the loud drugged or drunken youth straying through the purlieus of its bus station, across pleasant Wight scenery to my home in passably vibrant Victorian Ventnor and on along coastal charms and less

interesting matters to Ryde, decaying Victorian and Edwardian and even Art Deco splendour of undoubtedly melancholy aura to hideous and boarded-up modernity.

I do not admire the buses particularly, save only that among them are 1665 and 1666, these numbers equalling the dates of The Great Plague and Fire of London. Should I add 1667, the less well-known date of the Dutch fleet successfully invading the Medway?

I suspect, even while I do not particularly fear, that while I may not ever discover what the merry country lads had in mind on the question of Old John Braddle-um's number three, I must surely sooner or later pay attention to the matter therein of number five. ∎

Incredible, perhaps, that this scene of vehicles in regular daily service was little more than half a century ago. The Parisian Renault TN4F was already 35 years old, and of a profile which was not too different from that introduced in 1916. All this was to change a couple of months later, in June 1970, when the last were withdrawn. No 3267, third in this scene at Porte Pouchet, was then to transfer to her new owner in England, whereafter for the next 50 years the terms "Paris Bus" and "Robert Jowitt" became – for better or worse – largely synonymous.